Better Homes and Gardens®

RUG MAKING

BETTER HOMES AND GARDENS® BOOKS

Editor: Gerald Knox
Art Director: Ernest Shelton
Associate Art Director: Randall Yontz
Production and Copy Editors:
David Kirchner, Paul S. Kitzke
Crafts Editor: Nancy Lindemeyer
Senior Crafts Editor — Books: Joan Cravens
Associate Crafts Editor: Ann Levine
Senior Graphic Designer: Harijs Priekulis
Rug Making Designer: Neoma Alt West
Graphic Designers: Faith Berven,
Sheryl Veenschoten, Rich Lewis, Linda Ford

CONTENTS

Put your fabric scraps to work by making one of the braided or rag rugs shown in this section. Because you use recycled materials and need no special equipment, these rugs are just as economical as they are attractive and durable.

Even if you are a novice with a crochet hook or knitting needles, you will find these rugs a cinch to make. Knowledge of just a few basic stitches will give you the spectacular results shown in this section.

There's no guesswork when making a hooked or needlepoint rug; either the pattern is drawn onto the backing fabric or you work directly from a charted design. Either way, the rug appears precisely as it did on the pattern. Take your pick of punch-hook, latch-hook, or quickpoint designs, all included in this section.

Special Rug-Making Techniques ___ 56-77

Variety is the name of the game with these unusual and creative hand-made rugs. Each uses a style, technique, or material that sets it apart from other designs and ideas. Included are imaginative projects like a tie-dyed rug, rugs made on sewing machines, and a felt appliqué rug.

Creative Rug Making _____ 78-95

After learning the most common rug-making techniques, it's time to expand your knowledge of basic skills and try the unique designs shown here. Although not necessarily more difficult, they will give you an idea of how creative rug making can be.

Credits and Acknowledgments _____96

Rag & Braided Rugs

There is something wonderfully special about a handmade rug that is warm and appealing and beautiful, however humble its origins. So what nicer way is there to begin our book than with the traditional braid shown here—a genuinely happy marriage of practicality and big impact! And in the rest of our collection, you'll find a terrific selection of rugs to make in a wide variety of techniques and materials—all with easy-to-follow instructions.

To learn to make a braided rug, please turn the page.

6

How to Make a Braided Rug

What could be more inviting than a soft, warm, and homey braided rug in front of the fire? Or a splendid room-size braid in your dining room? Each can be a wonderfully personal and creative addition to your home.

And you can take pride in your practicality, too, for braided rugs are virtually no-cost. Just gather up used clothing and sewing scraps, cut them into strips, and braid them into a rug that's just the size you want. Here's all you need to know to get started.

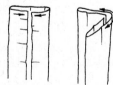

Folding Strips

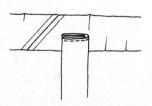

Joining Strips

Fabric and Equipment
The scrap basket is the rug crafter's treasure chest. Look there for worn clothing and remnants from sewing projects to make into rugs. And add to your cache by shopping at rummage sales and second-hand stores for suitable fabrics.

For a traditional braid, choose solid colors, tweeds, and patterns, keeping an eye on their dark and light values so you'll have an interesting mix of shades and textures.

Heavy- or medium-weight wools are best for really durable rugs, although lightweight wools work well in small rugs; cottons, linens, and blends are worth trying for their special effects. Knits, however, stretch so much that they're best avoided. Also avoid mixing light and heavy fabrics; they produce braids that wear unevenly and look lumpy.

Whatever you choose, opt for smooth, closely woven fabrics rather than loosely woven, rough, or loopy ones that may pull, snag, or catch a heel.

For equipment, turn to your sewing basket for safety pins, scissors, a thimble, heavy thread (such as carpet thread), tailor's chalk, and a yardstick. To join braids, use lacers (used to thread elastic) or curved carpet needles.

Estimating Fabric Needs
The amount of fabric needed depends on the size of the rug, the weight of the fabric, the width of the strips cut for braiding, and the tightness of the braid — it's a very individual thing. You can expect to lose between 1 to 2 feet of yardage for every 4 feet that you braid. For the best estimate, cut 3 strips the width you expect to use in your rug, each 2 yards long. Braid, and measure fin-

ished length and "uptake" to determine actual requirements.

Cutting Strips
When using old clothing, remove worn spots before cutting. Also remove collars, cuffs, pockets, zippers, and buttons. Open seams.

Cut fabric into strips 2 to 4 inches wide, depending on the weight of the fabric and the desired thickness of the rug. Generally, heavy fabrics are cut narrower than light ones.

Cut or tear strips on the straight grain to minimize stretching. Use a yardstick and chalk to mark cutting lines.

Piecing Strips Together
To simplify braiding, join strips together into 10- to 12-foot lengths using one of the methods illustrated on page 20. The slit-knot method is less satisfactory, though, because raw edges may show. With the "shortcut" method, end each cut of the fabric a distance from the edge equal to the width of the strip. For example, on a 2-inch strip, stop cutting 2 inches short of the edge.

Hiding Raw Edges
Fold strips in half lengthwise so raw edges meet in the center; then fold strips in half, as shown at left. Roll each strip into a ball.

Braiding
Begin by unwrapping 4 feet from three balls. Join two strips on the bias, then add a third strip to form a "T," as shown at left. Anchor joined ends to a chair or doorknob.

Braid by bringing the left strip over the middle strip (either by twisting or folding it over). Then bring the right strip over the middle strip, as in the diagram opposite.

The Traditional Braid *(shown on pages and 4 and 5)*

Directions

Note: The finished size of the oval braid shown on pages 4 and 5 is 76x90 inches. To make it, you'll need approximately 25 yards of 44-inch-wide dress-weight woolen yardage or the equivalent in worn clothing and sewing remnants. Adjust fabric estimates for a larger or smaller rug accordingly.

Review the general instructions opposite and below and then select and prepare fabrics for cutting. Cut them into 2½-inch-wide strips and join strips into 3- or 4-yard lengths. Fold strips to hide raw edges and roll them into balls or fold into bundles. To begin, join three strips into a "T" as shown opposite, and braid following the diagram below.

When joining and braiding strips, keep in mind the arrangement of shades, colors, and patterns because a pleasing variation will add much to the beauty of your rug. Refer to the photograph on pages 4 and 5 for ideas, if necessary.

Start shaping the rug around an 18-inch length of braid. This strip forms the center of the rug. If you wish to make your oval rug a different size, determine the length of the starter (center) strip by subtracting the width of your planned rug from its length. For example, for a 3x4-foot rug, the starter strip should be one foot long (4−3=1).

Lace braided strips together as you work, with lacers or a curved needle and thread, following the instructions below.

To care for your braided rug, shake it vigorously to remove loose dirt and have it professionally cleaned when necessary. Use rug beaters with care because they tend to loosen the fibers in a rug and may snag the braids.

Our pioneer ancestors knew the virtue of saving every small scrap of fabric – and the joy of crafting them into useful objects for their homes. Our oval braid is just such a project – easy and economical to make, sturdy and long-wearing, and enormously satisfying to own.

Materials

Wool from worn clothing, or
  new yardage (see note)
Carpet thread
Curved carpet needle or lacers

How to Make a Braided Rug *(continued)*

Keep tension even and avoid stretching the braid. At the end of each 10- to 12-foot length, stitch new strips to working strips and continue braiding. Stagger seams a bit to avoid lumps in the braid.

Shaping the Braid

As you work, shape the braided strips into the rug and lace them together. Starting with the joined end of the braid, begin coiling it into a circle, square, or rectangle. As you progress, gradually wind the entire braid into this shape. Be sure circles are rounded and squares have corners.

To start an oval, see directions above for the traditional braid on pages 4 and 5.

Lacing

Lace braids together side by side using a carpet needle or lacers and heavy thread.

Anchor the thread and draw it through the loop of one braid. Then thread it through the closest loop of the neighboring braid, as shown at right. Work back and forth between braids until they are secure.

Braids should remain flat; do not wind or lace too tightly.

Tapering

Taper the ends of the braid for a smooth finish on the edge of the rug. Cut the final 18 inches to about half the normal width, braid, and slip the ends into a loop of the adjacent coil. Slip-stitch so no raw edges show.

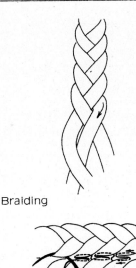

Braiding

Lacing

Braiding in the Round

Can braiding be a lap craft? You bet it can with a project as quick, easy, and imaginative as this one. To make a large, room-size rug, all you need to do is create lots of "small" rugs – rounds measuring 13 inches in diameter. Join them all together (with small rounds fitted in) to make a six-by-seven-foot rug.

By varying the number of rounds, you can easily make a rug to fit any spot in your house. And if you get family and friends to help with the work – as in the photograph on page 11 – you'll have your rug in short order.

Materials

Approximately 7 yards of 44-inch-wide, smooth, closely woven medium-weight wool in a variety of colors, patterns, and tweeds for the center section (see note)
3 yards yellow wool (see note)
4½ yards red wool (see note)
5½ yards blue wool (see note)
Carpet thread
Lacer or blunted carpet needle

Directions

Note: Yardage requirements are approximate because the precise amount depends on the weight of the fabric, the width of the strips, and the tightness of the braid. One yard of 44-inch-wide fabric yields 25 yards of 1¾-inch strips.

The center of the rug is about 3½x4½ feet and is made of twelve 13-inch rounds and six 3- to 3½-inch rounds. They are braided in assorted colors and patterns using strips of woolen remnants and scrap basket fabrics equal to about 7 yards of material. A continuous red braid outlines the center.

Unifying the design is a border of 18 large rounds worked in primary colors. Fourteen blue rounds fit between them.

Review the general instructions on pages 6 and 7. Then prepare old clothing and scraps for cutting. Cut fabric into strips 1¾ inches wide. If fabric is lightweight, cut strips a little wider; if it is heavy, cut them a little narrower.

Piece strips together into 4-yard lengths (for large rounds), and roll each into a ball.

You may wish to braid border rounds first, then braid any leftover border strips into the center rounds.

For each large round, use three 4-yard strips. Fold under raw edges and join short ends of strips into a "T." Anchor the ends of the strips and braid.

Taper the end of each braid so it will blend smoothly with the edge of the round.

To make the rounds, tuck the beginning end of the braid into a circle and lace with carpet thread. Shape the braid into a larger and larger circle, lacing as you go, as shown in the photograph on page 10. (Lacing instructions are on page 7.)

continued

Braiding in the Round *(continued)*

At the edge of each braided round, tuck the tapered end of the braid into the folds of the braid adjacent to it. Stitch and lace it firmly in place.

Braid and coil smaller rounds — 3 to 3½ inches in diameter — in the same way, and fit them between large rounds.

Braid as many rounds as necessary to make desired size.

Arrange the finished rounds in rows, as shown in the photograph opposite, and lace them together where they touch. Join the large rounds first and then add the smaller ones.

Finish the inner section of the rug with a long, continuous solid-color braid laced around the perimeter, as shown in the photograph on pages 8 and 9. Then add the outer (border) rounds, lacing them firmly to each other.

Calico Patchwork

Here's a rug with country charm and city sophistication. A braided rug with a new twist, this classy-looking floor covering is worked in squares, patchwork-style. Braid one patch at a time, and then lace the braids together in accordion folds as shown in the diagram below.

Once you've made a few "patches," you can piece them together to use and enjoy while you finish the rest of the rug.

Fabric requirements are for the large, 54x108-inch rug shown here. To estimate fabric needs for a smaller or larger rug, figure about one yard each of three different prints for each 18-inch square.

Materials
20 yards yellow cotton calico
18 yards red cotton calico
9 yards blue cotton calico
9 yards green cotton calico
Carpet thread
Rubber bands or twist ties
Blunt tapestry needle

Directions

Note: This rug is made of eighteen 18-inch squares — nine red, yellow, and blue ones and nine red, yellow, and green ones. Vary the size of your rug by altering the number of squares. The finished size also will depend on the weight of the fabric used and the tightness of the braid.

To prepare strips for braiding, cut the fabric along the lengthwise grain into 3-inch-wide strips about 5 yards long. Sew short lengths together in ¼-inch bias seams.

Press under raw edges of each strip about ¼ inch and fold strips in half lengthwise, as shown in the diagram on page 6. Fold strips into small bundles and secure with twist ties or rubber bands. When braiding, pull ends of strips from the bundles.

For each braided square, join two strips in a bias seam and attach a third strip to make a "T," referring to pages 6 and 7 for specific instructions. Braid the strips in combinations of red, yellow, and green, and red, yellow, and blue. Keep the folded edges of each strip in the center of the braid and keep tension even as you work. Do not taper the strips at the end of the braid for each square; instead, stitch them together, tucking in raw edges.

To make each square, fold the braid back and forth in 18-inch lengths and lace the lengths together side-by-side with carpet thread (see the diagram below). Draw the thread through a loop in one braid and then through the corresponding loop in the braid adjacent to it. Braids should lie flat. Make each braided "patch" 18 inches square. Make nine squares with blue strips and nine squares with green strips.

To assemble the rug, arrange the squares in rows three squares wide and six squares long. Turn every other square so the braids alternate running horizontally and vertically (see the diagram below). Also alternate blue squares with green squares. Lace squares firmly together.

Cut 4-inch-wide yellow bias strips and sew the strips together to make a binding for the rug. Press the raw edges under ¼ inch and fold the strip in half lengthwise. Slip-stitch the binding to the edge of the rug.

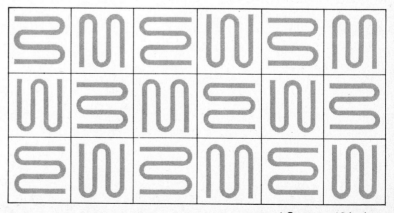

1 Square = 18 Inches

"Shag" Rag Rugs:
Scrap Bag Scatter Rug

Every scrap in your basket will find a place in this fun, fluffy rug. Just cut or tear each one into strips and knot them into a backing of monk's cloth. And if all the materials are preshrunk and machine-washable, the rug will be as easy to care for as it is to make.

Materials
Assorted cotton and cotton/
  polyester fabric scraps
24x40 inches monk's cloth or
  other fabric
1-inch-wide hem tape
Assorted 1- to 1½-inch-wide
  ribbon scraps
Blunt, large-eyed tapestry
  needle

Directions
Cut or tear fabric into strips 1 to 1½ inches wide. Make sure the strips follow the straight grain of the fabric. Each strip should be about 12 inches long, but do not worry about being exact because lengths should vary slightly. Do not fold or turn the raw edges on each strip; ragged edges add a nice homespun texture to the rug.

Fold the hem tape in half lengthwise and sew it to the edges of the fabric, binding them. This gives the backing a finished edge and prevents raveling.

Thread the strips one at a time through the needle. Starting in the center of the fabric, attach each strip to the backing by taking a small stitch, leaving both ends on the front. Make sure the ends of the strip are even, and tie them in a square knot. Leave the ends long and floppy.

Repeat this procedure for all the strips, working from the center of the fabric to the edge. Intermingle ribbon with fabric scraps, and mix colors at random. Fill the entire rug with strips, making sure no backing shows. Densely cover the backing so the finished rug is full and fluffy. Wash the rug in a gentle machine cycle when necessary, and hang to dry. Shake frequently to remove loose dirt particles.

"Shag" Rag Rugs *(continued)*
Recycled Denim

What better way is there to sneak a little more wear from old blue jeans than with this terrific little scatter rug? Cut jeans — and scraps of red fabric, too — into narrow strips and knot them into rug canvas with a latch-hooking tool.

Materials
2 pairs light blue adult-size
    denim jeans
2 pairs dark blue adult-size
    denim jeans
1 pair red denim jeans or ¼
    yard red linen
21x28 inches #4-count
    penelope canvas
Latch hook
Waterproof marking pen
1½-inch-wide rug binding tape
Large needle and heavy thread

Color Key
Dark blue   DB
Light blue   LB
Red   R

Directions
Enlarge the design and transfer it to rug canvas using a water-proof pen. Allow a 1-inch border around each side for the hem. Bind the raw edges of the canvas with masking tape.

Cut jeans into 2½-inch-wide strips, avoiding the use of any pant seams. Cut each jean strip into ⅛-inch-wide pieces (so each piece measures ⅛x2½ inches).

Begin hooking at the bottom of the canvas, working completely across each row and toward the top. To make each knot, hold the hook in either hand and fold one strip around the base of the hook *below* the latchet bar, making sure ends are even. Push the hook into an open space and up through the space above it. (See the diagram on page 44 if necessary.) The latchet bar should be open. Place both strip ends into the hook (inside the latchet bar) with your other hand, making sure the ends are on the same side of the latchet. Pull the hook back so the latchet bar closes around the strip; let go of the strip. To tighten knots, tug the ends.

To finish, fold under the 1-inch border on the sides. Next, fold under the top and bottom borders; baste all margins to the rug back. Sew binding to the canvas, starting in the center of one side and keeping as close to the first row of knots as possible. Then sew binding to the back of the rug. Miter corners where the canvas overlaps, making sure each corner is secure. (If canvas has selvage edges, just sew them directly to the back of the rug; they do not need binding.)

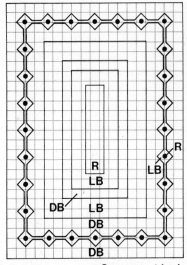

1 Square = 1 Inch

Cross-Stitch Alphabet Rug

If creative stitchery is your thing, you'll love this unusual "needlepoint" rug made with fabric instead of yarn. Work 2-inch-wide strips of fabric onto a canvas backing in simple cross-stitches for a rug that's wonderfully soft and sturdy.

If this 4x6-foot rug is more than you want to take on right now, why not try this exciting technique on a smaller rug, using the alphabet below to spell out your child's name, initials, or a favorite saying?

Materials

48x72-inch piece of #4-count penelope canvas (see note at right)

Twenty-six ½- to ¾-yard pieces of 45-inch-wide cotton fabric in assorted reds and blues for letters

4 double-bed-size white sheets for background

9 yards 45-inch-wide blue fabric for border

2 yards burlap for backing

Large-eyed tapestry needle

Waterproof marking pen

Masking tape

Carpet thread

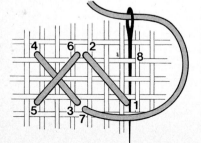

Directions

Note: If 48-inch-wide canvas is unavailable, buy 3½ yards of 36-inch-wide canvas, cut it in half, and piece it together by cutting off the selvage edges and overlapping the two pieces of canvas 1 inch. Whipstitch the two pieces together.

Bind the edges of the canvas with masking tape to prevent raveling. Pre-shrink the fabric and tear it into 2x45-inch strips.

Turn under the raw edges of the strips by folding and pressing each strip into thirds lengthwise. Use plastic bags to keep fabric clean, and keep the three different sets of fabric separate (letters, background, and borders).

With a waterproof pen, mark the center of the canvas by counting squares. Outline each letter on the canvas as shown on the pattern below. Each square represents one cross-stitch and each cross-stitch covers three horizontal and vertical threads. Keep the pattern centered by marking the inner letters first.

After outlines are complete, work the cross-stitches, referring to the stitch diagram, if necessary. Count the stitches carefully to make sure each stitch covers three threads of canvas. This will keep the pattern aligned.

To begin the cross-stitches, thread the needle with a strip of folded fabric and work the canvas the same way you would with rug yarn. Work half-cross-stitches across the canvas in one direction. Then cross them by working back across the canvas in the opposite direction, as shown in the diagram at left. Begin and end the stitches on the back side of the canvas, slipping the loose end through 2 or 3 stitches to secure it. Clip the ends.

Work the letters first, then the background, and finally the border. When finished, trim excess canvas around rug to 1 inch and blindstitch the edges to the back of the rug with carpet thread.

To back the rug, trim burlap to size, adding a 1-inch seam allowance. Turn under raw edges and whipstitch to border.

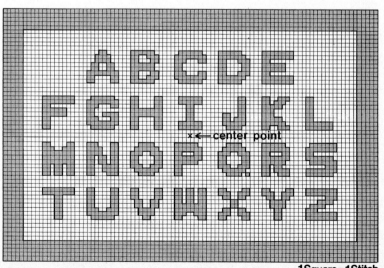

1 Square = 1 Stitch

Contemporary Crocheted Rug

With one easy crochet stitch and a few simple techniques, you can make a rag rug to rival anything that Grandmother used to make. And while the techniques are traditional, the look is "today" when this rug is worked in a variety of fabrics in related colors. Stitch and how-to diagrams are on page 20.

Materials

Sufficient new or used cotton or cotton-blend fabrics for the rug (see note at right)
Size J crochet hook

Directions

Note: Collect rags for the rug by culling old clothes, worn sheets, and other fabrics that are either all cotton or cotton blends. To color-scheme a rug like the one shown opposite, select a good mix of solid colors, patterns, prints, and checks. Ours is worked in blue and white fabrics and is about 8 feet in diameter. A rug about 3 to 4 feet in diameter requires about 9 yards of 45-inch-wide fabric (or the equivalent in salvaged materials). One yard of 45-inch fabric, sheet-weight, yields about 44 yards of 1-inch strips (accounting for seams).

Cut or tear fabric into strips ¾ to 1½ inches wide, depending on its weight. Tear heavy fabrics into ¾-inch strips, medium-weight fabrics into 1-inch strips, and light fabrics into 1½-inch strips. Cut all strips of any given fabric the same width.

Following the diagrams on page 20, join strips by sewing along the bias (diagonal); trim seams. Or join them by folding one end of one strip (A) over 1 inch. Cut ½ inch into the fold, centering the cut in the strip. Fold and cut the other strip (B) in the same way. Insert the cut end of B into the cut end of A, with the right sides of the strips facing the same direction.

Next, slide the uncut end of B through the slit, forming a loop. Gently pull the strip all the way through, at the same time tucking the short end of A through the slit in B. Make sure the joint remains flat. Repeat for all strips. Roll long, connected strips into large balls, as shown in the photograph below.

Work the rug by following the stitch diagrams on page 20. Make a slipknot and 6 chain stitches in one fabric strip (1). Join
continued

Contemporary Crocheted Rug *(continued)*

1 Chain stitching

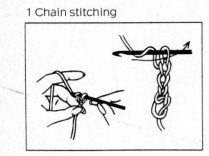

2 Slip-stitch into a ring

3 Single crochet

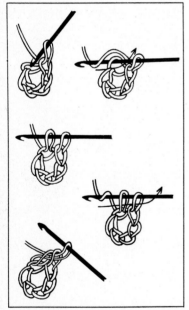

4 Increasing

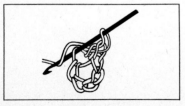

Joining fabric strips

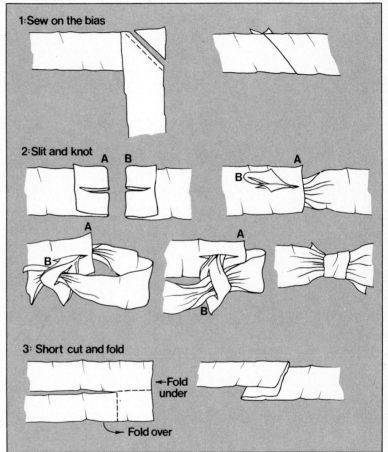

1: Sew on the bias

2: Slit and knot

A   B   A   B

A   A   B   B

3: Short cut and fold

←Fold under

← Fold over

them into a ring with a slip-stitch (2). In the first stitch of the ring, work a single crochet stitch (3). Then work another single crochet in the same stitch so it increases (4). Repeat this procedure in all 6 stitches of the ring.

Thereafter, continue single-crocheting (3), increasing in every other stitch for the second row and thereafter as necessary to maintain the rug's circular shape and flatness.

To change colors or add new strips, join a new strip to the preceding one by hand (by stitching two pieces together along the bias or by slit-joining as shown above). Continue single-crocheting, increasing occasionally and changing colors wherever you choose, until the rug is the desired size.

To finish the rug, cut the last 3 or 4 yards of fabric strips narrower (decreasing to about ⅜ inch wide at the end) so the last round of the rug will decrease in width, ending smoothly. Coat with soil repellent and launder in a heavy-duty machine.

Old-Fashioned Throw Rug

This delightful rug proves that there are no hard-and-fast rules about fabrics for rug making. It's made from an unusual assortment of dress-weight materials, including satin, jersey, and faille, that are transformed into a charming blend of colors and patterns when crocheted into this simple rectangular shape.

Our rug is 28x57 inches. To make yours a different size, see the how-to instructions for the traditional braid on page 7 to determine the length of the starter strip.

Materials

Assorted dress-weight fabrics and scraps in a variety of colors, prints, and textures equivalent to about 9 yards of 44-inch-wide fabric (for a rug with an area of 10 to 12 square feet)
Size J crochet hook

Directions

Prepare fabric for cutting, following directions on page 6. Cut strips 1 inch wide and join.

Fold strips to hide raw edges, following directions on page 6. Roll strips into balls.

To make a center, starter strip for the rug, ch 57, or until the strip is about 27 inches long. Follow diagrams opposite.

Crochet into back loops only.

Rnd 1: Starting with second ch from hook, sc in each loop of starter chain. At last loop on chain, make sharp corner by working sc, ch 1, sc, ch 1, sc all in last chain on strip. Work sc in loops of chain back to starting point, sc, ch 1, sc in same loop, sl st to join to last sc, ch 1.

Rnd 2: Sc in each st along the length, (sc, ch 1, sc) in corner ch 1 space, sc in end st(s), (sc, ch 1, sc) in next corner space, sc in each st along the length, (sc, ch 1, sc) in corner ch 1 space, sc in each end st(s), (sc, ch 1, sc) in corner ch 1 space, sl st to ch 1 to join at beg of rnd.

Rep rnd 2 until desired size.

Rugs to Knit and Crochet

Terrific techniques for floors—that's what you'll discover about crocheting and knitting in this section of our book. With materials like heavy yarns or cords and a crochet hook or knitting needles, you can create not only decorative rugs and runners in a wealth of patterns and textures, but also sturdy and practical floor coverings. The rug shown here, for example, is a popular granny square design worked in inexpensive yarns (directions are on the next page). And it's only one in a wonderful collection of patterns to knit and crochet—all calling for mastery of only a few basic stitches and procedures.

Granny Square Runner *(shown on pages 22 and 23)*

Simple granny squares make a spectacular rug when worked in a rainbow of colors and bordered in black, as shown in the rug on pages 22 and 23. For this 30x62-inch runner, crochet seventy-eight 4½-inch squares to join together into six rows of 13 squares each. To change the size of the rug, alter the number of squares or assemble them differently.

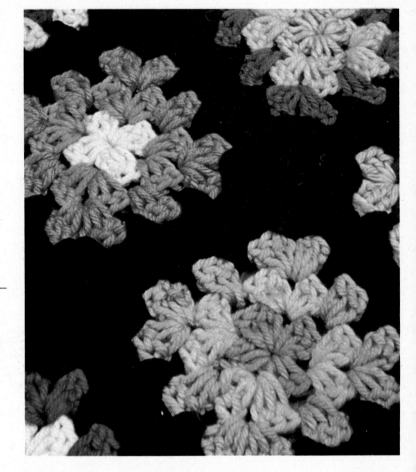

Materials
80-yard (2½-ounce) skeins of Belding Lily cotton rug yarn, or a suitable substitute, in the following colors and amounts: 14 black and 20 in assorted colors
Size I crochet hook

Gauge
1 square equals 4½ inches

Directions
Rnd 1: With any color, ch 4, sl st to form ring, ch 3 (counts as first dc), 2 dc in ring, ch 1, (3 dc in ring, ch 1) 3 times, sl st to top of ch 3. Fasten off.

Rnd 2: With another color, join in any corner sp, ch 3 (counts as first dc), 2 dc in corner sp, ch 1, 3 dc in corner sp, ch 1. Continue around square, making a 3 dc group in every sp of previous rnd *and* making a (3 dc, ch 1, 3 dc) group in every corner sp.

Rnd 3: Rep rnd 2, using different color.

Rnd 4: Rep rnd 2, using black yarn for each square.

Assembling — Make 78 squares. Crochet, weave, or sew the squares together, making six rows of 13, using black yarn.

Border — Attach black yarn anywhere along the outer edge, ch 1, make 1 sc in each dc and 1 sc in each joining st around. Do not make sc in sps between dc groups or border will not lie flat.

In corners, make 3 sc in corner sp, join to first ch with a sl st. Rep this rnd two more times using black yarn, change to a color for rnd 4, and finish with two more rnds of black. Fasten off.

Trim and weave in yarn ends.

Tips for Crocheting and Knitting Rugs

General Tips

Always buy enough yarn to complete your knitted or crocheted rug, and make sure the dye lot of each skein is the same, since dye lots vary and colors may be a shade different.

Familiarize yourself with common terms and abbreviations (on pages 30 and 32) since pattern designers often assume that you know how to work the details. For a review of the basic stitches, see pages 34 and 35.

Before you begin a rug project, check the stitch gauge in the instructions. It specifies how many stitches per inch you should have using a specified crochet hook or knitting needle. Since the size of the rug is dependent upon this gauge, you must adjust your work to the given gauge or your finished rug will not be the size indicated in the instructions.

Since everyone does not knit or crochet with the same tension, it is important to check your gauge before you start working. To do so, cast on or chain about 20 stitches, using the recommended yarn and needles or hook. Work about 4 inches in the specified pattern. Bind or fasten off. Block the swatch (see directions below) and then measure it to see whether rows and stitches correspond to the required gauge.

If your stitch gauge is less than the one given in the instructions, try the next size smaller needles or hook, and again check your gauge. If your stitch gauge is greater (more stitches per inch), try larger needles or hook.

To achieve a handmade rather than a homemade look, block your finished items. Dampen the piece to be blocked by spraying or dipping in water. With rustproof pins, such as stainless steel macrame T-pins, pin the rug in its final shape to a smooth cloth-covered surface that's larger than the piece you're blocking. Allow it to dry slowly, out of sun and away from heat.

If you make a rug larger than 3x5 feet, plan to use a pad beneath it. This ensures a longer life and makes your rug less apt to skid and easier to vacuum.

For small rugs, use non-skid padding underneath, or sew rubber jar rings to the four corners.

Clean large handmade rugs the same way you would commercially-made rugs — either professionally or with a rug cleaner.

To care for small handmade rugs, wash or dry-clean, depending on whether the yarns are washable. When washing, however, use cold water and gentle machine action. Avoid tumble-drying with high heat.

Special Crocheting Tips

When crocheting, be sure the yarn is always put over the hook from back to front, and that the number of stitches per row remains consistent.

To change colors without knots, work up to the final step of a stitch. Then take up the new yarn and finish the last step with this color. Pull the yarn ends through to the wrong side of the rug and weave them into the back when the rug is completed.

Special Knitting Tips

When you are joining a new ball of yarn, join at the outer edge whenever possible. With the new strand, make a slip knot around the strand you are knitting with. Then move the slip knot up to the edge of work and continue knitting with the new strand.

When you are working with more than one color, always pick up the color you are about to use from underneath the dropped strand. This prevents holes as you are changing colors.

Crocheting and knitting are simple craft techniques that produce quick and versatile results. And because of the wide variety of patterns available, they are among the most popular members of the needlecraft family. Here are some tips to help you turn out professional-looking results every time you stitch.

Scatter Rugs

These small and homey hand-stitched rugs will add instant warmth to any room in the house. The crocheted rug on the left is worked in simple stitches even a beginner can master. And while ours measures about 30x53 inches, it can actually be made any size.

The 29x36-inch checker-board rug is a double knit worked on circular needles.

For an explanation of the abbreviations used, see pages 30 and 32. Stitch diagrams are on pages 34 and 35.

Crocheted Rug

Materials
Eight 70-yard skeins Aunt Lydia's Italian blue rug yarn (A)
Eight 70-yard skeins Aunt Lydia's rust rug yarn (B)
Four 70-yard skeins Aunt Lydia's parchment rug yarn (C)
Two 70-yard skeins Aunt Lydia's medium blue rug yarn (D)
Size I aluminum crochet hook

Gauge
4 dc=1 inch, 10 rows=6 inches

Directions
Note: To make the rug a different size, adjust yarn amounts.

With 1 strand color A, ch 111.

Row 1: Work 2 dc in second ch from hook, 1 dc in each of next 3 ch, sk 2 ch, * 1 dc in each of next 4 ch, 3 dc in next ch, 1 dc in each of next 4 ch, sk 2 ch, rep from * to last 4 ch. Work 1 dc in each of next 3 ch, 2 dc in last ch. Ch 2, turn.

Row 2: Work 2 dc in 3rd loop from hook, 1 dc in each of next 3 dc, sk 2 dc, * 1 dc in each of next 4 dc, 3 dc in next dc, 1 dc in each of next 4 dc, sk 2 dc, rep from * across to last 4 dc. Work 1 dc in each of next 3 dc, 2 dc in last dc. Ch 2, turn.

Rep row 2 for pattern. Work 2 more rows A, 2 rows B, 1 row C, 1 row D, 1 row C, 2 rows B. Rep these 11 rows for entire rug, ending with 4 more rows A.

Clip ends and weave into work.

Knitted Rug

Materials
Seven 70-yard skeins Aunt Lydia's burnt orange rug yarn
Seven 70-yard skeins Aunt Lydia's navy rug yarn
Size 10½ circular knitting needle
Size I aluminum crochet hook
10 ring markers

Gauge
3 sts=1 inch on one side (6 sts of double knit)

Directions
Note: In addition to the basic knitting stitches, you will need to know yf (bring yarn forward), yb (take yarn back), pso (pass stitch over), and pw (purlwise, or as if to purl).

Pattern — double-knit with one color for practice: A: * k 1 (yf), sl 1 (pw) *, rep * to * every row (this gives st st face). B: * k 1 (yb), sl 1 (pw) *, rep * to * every row (for garter st face).

As an exercise, you can make a potholder by casting on 42 sts. Divide into units of 14 sts; * work A for 14 sts, B for 14 sts, A for 14 sts *, rep * to * to desired size.

Pattern for double knit with two colors:

Group No. 1 (first side).

Block No. 1 (navy st st face) —A: * k 1 navy (yf), p 1 orange (yb) *, rep for 18 sts, slip ring to right needle, take navy (yb), orange (yf).

Block No. 2 (orange garter st face) — B: * p 1 orange, k 1 navy *, rep for 14 sts, slip ring to right needle, orange (yb).

Group No. 1 (second side).

Block No. 1 (orange st st face) — C: * k 1 orange (yf), p 1 navy (yb) *, rep for 18 sts, navy (yf), orange (yb).

Block No. 2 (navy garter st face) — D: * p 1 navy, k 1 orange *, rep for 14 sts, navy (yb).

Rep group No. 1 until there are 12 ridges of garter st in orange (block No. 2).

Group No. 2 (first side).

Block No. 1 (orange garter st face) — orange (yf), navy (yb) —E: * k 1 navy, p 1 orange *, rep for 18 sts.

Block No. 2 (navy st st face) —F: * p 1 orange (yb), navy (yb) k 1, (yf) *, rep for 14 sts.

Group No. 2 (second side).

Block No. 1 (navy garter st face) — G: * k 1 orange (yb), p 1 navy (yf) *, rep for 18 sts, orange (yf).

Block No. 2 (orange st st face) — H: * p 1 navy (yb), k 1 orange (yf) *, rep for 14 sts, end with orange (yb), navy (yf).

Rep Group No. 2 until there are 8 orange ridges on each of the sides.

To begin, *cast on* in two colors using two end of yarn method:

First square: * start with orange (1st st), navy 2nd st), pull 2 orange ends between 2 navy ends and cast on orange, pull orange between 2 navy ends and cast on navy *, rep for 18 sts ending in navy, put on marker.

Second square: * cast on navy, pull navy between orange and cast on orange, pull navy between orange and cast on navy *, rep for 14 sts, ending with orange.

Rep above two blocks 5 times, rep 1st block. This gives you 178 sts on needle.

Follow directions for Groups 1 and 2, rep 7 times, rep Group No. 1, cast off with navy.

To cast off, * k 2 tog, k 2 tog, pso *, rep to end. Cut yarn and pull end through loop. Use this method with one or more colors of yarn.

At each end of rug, work one row of navy single crochet.

For fringe, use four 20-inch lengths of yarn. At each corner, pull 4 ends of orange through, knot the 8 ends tog. At either side of orange, rep with navy. Trim the fringe to desired length.

"Parquet" Rug

Even traditional crochet patterns take on a new look when worked in natural jute – a stunning, contemporary alternative to yarn. These 12-inch blocks work up quickly and easily with only two stitches. Assemble the completed squares according to the diagram below for a parquet look.

For stitch abbreviations and diagrams, please see pages 30 and 34.

Materials
Size J crochet hook
Natural, unbleached 3-ply raw jute (amount depends on size of rug and how tightly you crochet. Work up a sample square and calculate needs accordingly)

Directions
The rug pictured here consists of 27 single-crocheted squares, 27 double-crocheted squares, and 26 squares of alternating rows of single and double crochet. There are 80 squares in all, each measuring 12 inches square.

The finished rug is approximately 8x10 feet, including the scalloped crocheted border added to the short ends of the rug. The squares are arranged in a parquet pattern (see below, left) to give the rug more texture and reduce stretching.

1. *Single-crochet square:* Work 16 rows of single crochet, 20 stitches per row. Make 27 squares.

2. *Double-crochet square:* Work 8 rows of double crochet, 21 stitches per row. Make 27 squares.

3. *Single/double-crochet square:* Work, alternating 6 rows of single and 5 rows of double crochet, 21 stitches per row. Make 26 squares.

Note: Because you are working with raw jute, the yarn will vary in width and bulkiness, and hence there might be slight differences in the size of each square. Squares can be stretched and blocked to uniform size before joining.

4. *To finish ends of squares:* Cut the two end strings and, using crochet hook, tuck ends under three or four stitches. Tuck both ends under on the same side of square (this will be the wrong side of the rug).

5. *Stitching squares together:* Squares are laid out in a parquet pattern. Arrange squares in ten rows of eight squares each, alternating among the three patterns (single, double, and single/double) and alternating the *direction* of each square (see the photograph opposite and the

diagram below for pattern arrangement).

Join squares together using chain stitches. To avoid numerous bulky loose ends, join two squares together and then, without cutting yarn, move on to the next two squares. Continue until you have joined eight pairs of squares in a row.

End yarn and weave back into rug. Next, join a row of eight more squares to the original set of eight pairs. Proceed until all squares are joined horizontally.

Finally, join squares along vertical rows. Clip yarns and use crochet hook to work loose ends back into the wrong side of the rug so none of the ends show.

6. *To finish rug:* Circle the entire rug with a row of single crochet.

a. Add another row of single crochet to one of the sides with eight squares.

b. To make scallop trim, sc through first stitch on the edge of the rug.

c. Next st is a dc, which will join the first sc with the fourth stitch along border of rug. This fourth stitch will be the center of the scallop, and you will crochet five more double-crochet stitches through this stitch (each scallop thus has a total of six double-crochet stitches).

d. The sixth double-crochet stitch will then be joined by a chain stitch to the seventh single-crochet stitch of the border.

Repeat from *step a* to make scallops along one entire side of rug. You should have about 28 scallops on one side. Repeat procedure for scallop trim on opposite side of rug. Gently steam-press finished rug.

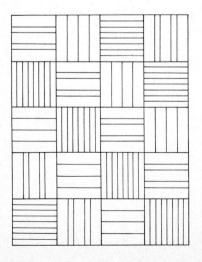

Quick-and-Easy Jute Rug

Here's another traditional crochet pattern – the scallop – looking chic in natural fibers. Heavy, five-ply jute cord in three colors works up quickly into a beautifully textured 45x72-inch rug.

This great contemporary look is simple to stitch, too – it's worked entirely in single crochet. (For diagrams of this stitch, see page 34).

To minimize shedding while working with jute, wind each color into balls and store them in plastic bags.

Materials
540 yards brown 5-ply jute
540 yards bleached white 5-ply jute
190 yards rust 5-ply jute
Size K crochet hook

Directions
Ch 142 with brown jute.

Row 1: 1 sc in second ch from hook and in each of next three ch, 3 sc in next ch, * 1 sc in each of next 4 ch, sk next two ch, 1 sc in each of next 4 ch, 3 sc in next ch; rep from *, ending 1 sc in each of last 4 ch. Ch 1, turn.

Row 2: Sk first sc, 1 sc in each of next 4 sc, 3 sc in next sc, * 1 sc in each of next 4 sc, sk next 2 sc, 1 sc in each of next 4 sc, 3 sc in next sc; rep from *, ending 1 sc in each of next 3 sc, sk next sc, 1 sc in last sc. Ch 1, turn. Rep Row 2 for pat, changing to rust jute for Rows 7 and 8. Rows 9 through 14 are worked in bleached white jute.

Rep entire procedure three more times.

To block finished rug, steam-press so the entire rug lies flat. Shake or beat the rug periodically to remove dirt (5-ply jute will withstand occasional beating).

Crochet Abbreviations
beg . . . . begin(ning)
ch . . . . chain
dc . . . . . double crochet
dec . . . . decrease
dtr . . . . . . double treble
hdc . . . . half double crochet
inc . . . . increase
lp(s) . . . . loop(s)
pat . . . . pattern
rnd . . . . round
sc . . . . . . single crochet
sl st . . . . slip stitch
sp . . . . space
st(s) . . . . stitch(es)
tog . . . . together
yo . . . . yarn over

Knitted Patchwork Rug

Deep tones mixed with white make this rug a refreshing accent for your floor. Knit two colors together into 12-inch squares, join them patchwork-style, and surround them all with a wide border.

Materials

70-yard skeins of heavy-duty rug yarn in the following amounts and colors: 32 off-white, 4 cerise, 6 yellow, 5 chartreuse, and 17 turquoise.
Size 11 knitting needles.
Tapestry needle.

Measurements for Blocking

Approximately 4½ x 6½ feet

Knitting Abbreviations

beg	begin(ning)
CC	contrasting color
dec	decrease
dp	double-pointed
inc	increase
k	knit
MC	main color
p	purl
pat	pattern
psso	pass slip st over
rem	remaining
rep	repeat
rnd	round
sk	skip
sl st	slip stitch
sp	space
st(s)	stitch(es)
st st	stockinette stitch
tog	together
yo	yarn over
*	repeat from * as indicated

Directions

Make the rug of fifteen 12-inch squares sewn together with a 9-inch border around the edges. To change the size, alter the number of squares and the length of the borders.

Work the entire rug in garter stitch: knit every row.

To make each square, use one full skein each of white and a color, and knit the two together. The border requires about 3½ skeins each of white and turquoise for the short sides, and 5 skeins each for the long sides.

For squares, cast on 29 stitches using two strands of yarn; knit until the piece measures 12 inches. Make 15 knitted squares.

For borders, cast on 21 stitches using two strands of yarn. Knit two strips 36 inches long and two 78 inches long.

When squares are finished, arrange colors in a pleasing design such as the one shown below. Stitch them together with a tapestry needle threaded with a double strand of yarn. Add borders in the same way so all of the pieces are secure.

Whimsical Crocheted Rug

Bright colors trim the "petals" of this whimsical white flower blossom. And because it's worked in only one stitch, it's easier to "grow" than the real thing!

Work single-crochet rounds in three sizes and join them together to make this 38-inch rug.

For stitch abbreviations and diagrams, see pages 30 and 34.

Materials
13 skeins white 3-ply rug yarn
2 skeins green 3-ply rug yarn
1 skein red 3-ply rug yarn
1 skein yellow 3-ply rug yarn
Row markers
Tapestry needle
Size H crochet hook

Directions

18-inch center circle (make 1):

Rnd 1: With white yarn, ch 4, join with sl st to form ring.

Rnd 2: 8 sc in ring; do not join rounds but use a marker in first st worked to indicate beginning of round.

Rnd 3: * 2 sc in first sc, sc in next sc, repeat from *.

Rnds 4, 7, 9, and 11: Rep rnd 3.

Rnd 5: Sc in each sc around.

Rnds 6, 8, 10, 12, 13, 14, 16, and 17: Rep rnd 5.

Rnd 15: * 2 sc in first sc, sc in each of next 2 scs, rep from *.

Rnds 18 and 29: Rep rnd 15.

Rnds 19 through 28: Rep rnd 5.

Rnds 30 and 31: Sc in each sc, sl st in first sc and cut yarn.

9-inch white circles (make 9): Follow directions for large center circle for 17 rnds.

1½-inch green circles (make 9):

Follow directions for large center circle for 3 rnds.

To assemble the rug, position smaller white circles around the center circle as shown in the photograph. Using a tapestry needle and yarn, sew small circles to large one for a distance of seven stitches. Arrange small green circles between the nine white circles and sew in place. Then work edging.

Edging — Rnd 1: Attach red yarn in center sc at top of small green circle, sc in same sp, sc in each sc around.

Sew 7 sc between each circle so circles are joined.

For yellow edging, sc around, *except that at points where circles intersect* sk 3 sc. Complete 1 row. Rep for white (1 row) and green (2 rows).

End off; weave in end of yarn.

To block, steam lightly so rug lies flat. Machine-wash on gentle cycle when necessary.

Basic Crochet Stitches

Chain stitch

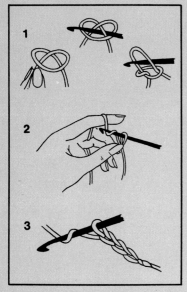

Start by making a slipknot on crochet hook about 6 inches from end of yarn (1). Pull one end of yarn to tighten knot. Hold hook between right index finger and thumb, as you would a pencil. Wrap yarn over ring finger, under middle finger, and over index finger, holding short end between thumb and index finger. For more tension, wrap yarn around little finger. Insert hook under and over strand of yarn (2). Make foundation chain by catching strand with hook and drawing it through loop (3). Make chain as long as pattern calls for.

Single crochet

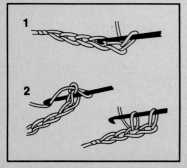

Single crochet, continued

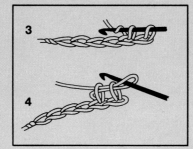

Insert hook into the second chain from hook, under two upper strands of yarn (1). Draw up a loop (2). Draw yarn over hook (3). Pull yarn through two loops, completing single crochet stitch (4). Insert hook into next stitch and repeat last four steps.

Half-double crochet

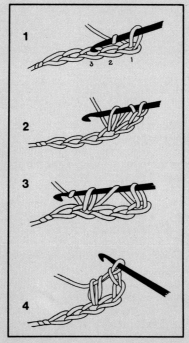

With yarn over hook, insert hook into third chain, under two upper strands of yarn (1). Draw up a loop (2). Draw yarn over hook (3) Pull through three loops, completing half-double crochet (4).

Double crochet

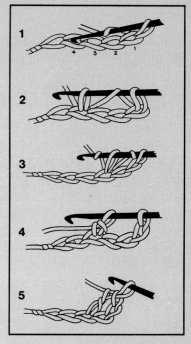

Holding yarn over hook, insert hook into fourth chain, under two upper strands of yarn (1). Draw up a loop (2). Wrap yarn over hook (3). Draw yarn through two loops (4). Yarn over again and draw through last two loops on hook (5) to complete.

Slip stitch

After you've made the foundation chain, insert the crochet hook under the top strand of the second chain from the hook and yarn over. With a single motion, pull the yarn through the stitch and loop on the hook. Insert the hook under the top strand of the next chain, then yarn over and draw the yarn through stitch and loop on hook. Repeat this procedure to the end of the chain.

Basic Knitting Stitches

Casting on

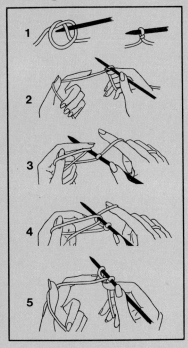

Make a slipknot around needle at a distance from yarn end that equals one inch for each stitch to be cast on (1). Hold needle with slipknot in your right hand and make a loop of the short length of yarn around your left thumb (2). Insert point of needle in your right hand under loop on left thumb (3). Loop yarn from ball over fingers of right hand (4). Wind yarn from ball under and over needle and draw it through loop, leaving the stitch on the needle (5). Tighten stitches on needle and bring yarn end around thumb. Repeat last four steps for desired number of stitches. Switch hands.

Knitting

Knitting, continued

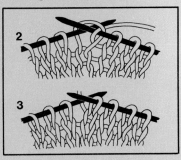

Hold needle with stitches in left hand and other needle in right hand. Insert right needle through stitch on left needle from front to back. Pass yarn around point of right needle to form loop (1). Pull this loop through stitch on left needle and draw loop onto right needle (2). Now slip the stitch completely off of the left needle (3). Repeat until you have transferred all stitches from left needle to right needle. This completes one row. When working the next row, move needle holding stitches to left hand, and other needle to right hand.

Purling

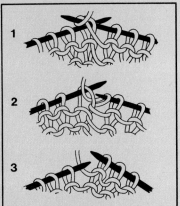

Hold the needle with the stitches in your left hand and the other needle in your right hand. Insert the right needle through the stitch on the left needle from back to front. Wind the yarn around the point of the right needle to form a loop (1). Draw a loop through the stitch on the needle in your left hand and transfer it to the needle in your right hand (2). Slip stitch completely off left needle (3). Repeat these steps until all loops are transferred to right needle.

Increasing & decreasing

In order to increase a stitch, knit or purl as usual, but do not slip it off left needle. Instead, insert right needle into back of stitch and knit or purl into stitch again, as shown. Slip both onto right needle, making two stitches.

To decrease, knit or purl two stitches together at the same time.

To slip a stitch, insert the right needle as if to purl (unless directions say as if to knit). Then slip stitch onto right needle without working or twisting.

Binding off

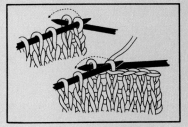

Work two stitches in pattern loosely. With left needle, lift first stitch over second stitch and off right needle. This binds off one stitch. Repeat for required number of stitches. To bind off a row, continue until one stitch remains; break yarn and draw end through last stitch.

Hooked & Needlepoint Rugs

When you needlepoint or hook a rug, you can create a field of flowers for your floor—such as the wildflower bouquet shown here—or any of dozens of other delightful designs. Working with these two techniques is different from making braided, knitted, or crocheted rugs in that you sketch your pattern right on the burlap or canvas backing. The design possibilities are limitless, from beautifully simple to wonderfully complex. The wildflower rug is hooked with a punch needle, and it's just one of our super patterns. To learn to make it, please turn the page.

How to Make a Hooked Rug

To hook a rug like the lovely wildflower design pictured on the preceding pages, you can use either a punch needle or latchet hook. Each tool, however, requires a different set of procedures, materials, and techniques, despite the fact that the end results are quite similar.

For a step-by-step guide to hooking with a punch needle, see the directions at right. For information on latch-hooking a rug, please see page 44.

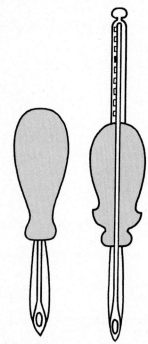

Punch-hooking tools

Materials and Equipment

Several kinds of punch-hooking tools are available for rug making. Some are equipped with needles in assorted sizes to accommodate anything from slender pearl cotton or linen threads up to the heaviest rug yarns. And some are adjustable to let you work everything from traditional low loops to long, rya-like loops for a shag look. In addition, there are several fast-action needles that make loops automatically as you turn the handle.

Choose the needle you find most comfortable and the one best suited to the yarn you plan to use, the design you are going to hook, and the speed with which you like to work.

Backing fabric holds the loops made by the needle. The weave must be tight enough to grip the loops, but loose enough to allow the needle to slip through easily.

Select a firm, long-wearing, even-weave fabric. Heavyweight burlap is popular because it is easy to work, readily available, and inexpensive.

Purchase enough fabric to allow a 3- to 6-inch margin around the design so that when it's mounted for hooking, the needle will not hit the frame.

A frame is essential when hooking a rug; the fabric must be taut or the hook will not work correctly. Use a purchased rug frame or make one from artist's stretcher strips or pieces of 1x2-inch lumber secured at the corners with C-clamps. Be sure corners are square and stable.

Estimating Yarn Requirements

To estimate yarn, see page 59.

Preliminary Steps

Begin by straightening the grain of the backing fabric and narrowly hemming the raw edges. Then transfer the design to the fabric, following directions on page 53. Be sure to reverse the pattern into a mirror image before transferring it since you will work from the back of the design. Finally, with the lengthwise grain of the fabric parallel to the sides of the frame and the design facing up, staple or overcast-stitch fabric tautly to frame.

Working the Design

To hook the design evenly, yarn must move freely through the needle. Thus, it's a good idea to rewind skeins of yarn into balls before beginning. Then thread the needle and adjust it for the length of the loops.

To begin hooking, hold the needle straight up and down over the canvas and push it completely into the fabric until the handle rests on the surface. (On the first stitch, the yarn tail will be on the face of the fabric; trim all tails even with loops after the rug is finished.) Raise the needle back up through the fabric until the tip just touches the fabric, then move it over a few threads for the next stitch. Work with the slot in the needle facing the direction in which you are hooking, and be sure the yarn flows freely. Continue as above, checking the face of the rug occasionally to be sure the pile is dense enough to cover backing.

As you work, outline small design areas first. Then fill them by hooking either in straight rows across each shape or in rows parallel to the outline, depending on the effect desired. The space between rows should be about the same as the space between loops. Hook the background last.

Loops may be left uncut or cut, as desired. If cut, they may be beveled to accent the design.

To finish the rug and secure yarn firmly to fabric after hooking, follow the directions on page 54.

Wildflower Bouquet *(shown on pages 36 and 37)*

Directions

Enlarge the pattern below and transfer it, centered, to backing fabric, following directions on page 53. Go over outlines with a waterproof pen so they are easy to see.

Tack backing fabric to a frame. With the punch-needle tool set to make a loop ½ inch long, fill in flowers, following directions opposite. Work the background last using green yarn.

When hooking is completed, coat the *punched area* of the back with liquid latex, following manufacturer's directions: Trim backing to within 4 inches of the hooked area. Thread tapestry needle with green yarn and sew a row of 4-inch loops ¾ inch from the punched edge using the rya knot stitch (see page 60 for directions). Sew another row of loops between the first one and the punched edge. Clip and trim loops to make a 3-inch fringe.

Turn the rug over and notch and trim the margin to 2½ inches. Apply a band of liquid latex at the edge and press the hem into it with your fingers, making sure it lies flat. Let dry thoroughly.

Low loops snugged close together make our wildflower rug a pleasing carpet of blooms. And its 44-inch size makes it large enough to bring the brilliance of springtime into your home.

Materials

60x60 inches burlap or punch-
   needle canvas
Rug punch tool
Rug frame
#13 tapestry needle
Embroidery transfer pencil
Waterproof pen
Staple gun
Liquid latex rug backing

Bucilla Multi-Craft Acrylic
  Rug Yarn (or its equivalent)
  in the following colors
   and amounts:
   A Forest green (20
     skeins)
   B Kelly green (3)
   C Dark violet (1)
   D Lemon yellow (1)
   E Sun-yellow (1)
   F Emerald green (1)
   G White (1)
   H Red-orange (1)
   I Light violet (1)
   J Brown (1)
   K Blue (1)
   L Pumpkin (1)
   M Medium magenta (1)
   N Dark Magenta (1)

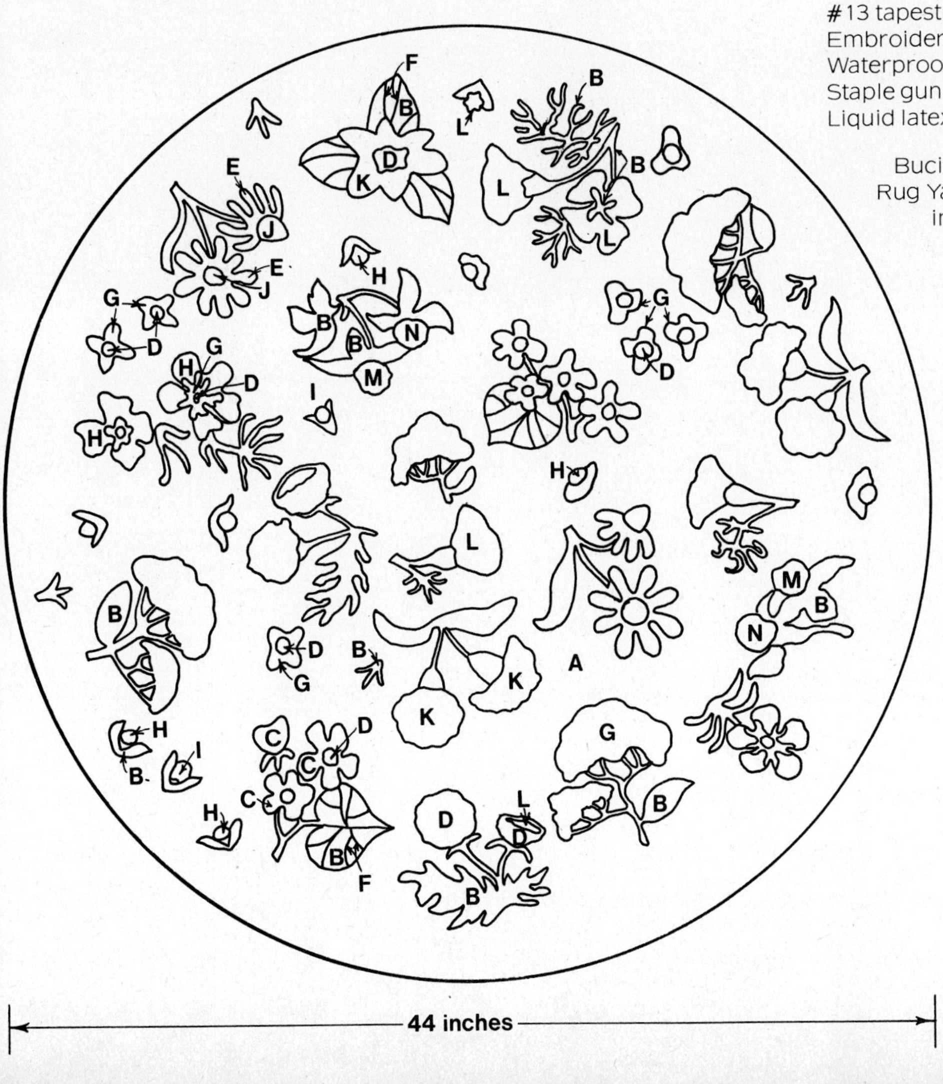

44 inches

Fantastical Animal Rug

This delightful child's rug is really four rugs in one. You can punch-hook each 24-inch block separately and then stitch them together into a square. Or, work just one in your child's favorite design to make a bath mat or a by-the-bed foot warmer.

Knitting yarns were used for this rug, but rug yarns work just as well.

Materials
4-ounce skeins knitting yarn in the following amounts and colors: 3 orange, 3 yellow, 2 scarlet, 1 emerald, 3 colonial blue, 1 black, and 1 purple
Four 27-inch squares heavy-duty burlap
Liquid latex rug backing
11 yards rug binding
Punch-needle tool
24x24-inch rug frame or artist's stretcher strips
Waterproof marking pen
1½-inch-wide paintbrush
Carpet thread

Color key
B Black
Bl Blue
G Green
O Orange
P Purple
R Red
Y Yellow

Directions
Note: If you wish to use rug yarn rather than knitting yarn, determine the yarn requirements by punching one square inch with the desired rug yarn. Then pull the stitches out and measure the length of yarn used. To determine how much more yarn you will need, figure how many square inches there are in each section of color.

Cut four 27-inch squares from the burlap. Enlarge and reverse the designs and transfer them, centered, to the wrong side of the burlap squares, following the directions on page 53. Go over outlines with a waterproof marking pen. Attach the squares to the frame one at a time with extra-long thumbtacks, making sure the burlap is taut.

Thread the punch-needle tool and adjust it for ¼-inch loops. Punch-hook the designs following the general instructions on page 38, leaving a 1½-inch border of unworked burlap along each side of each square. Make sure the loops are close enough together to cover the backing completely. Begin and end the yarn on the right side, leaving a long tail that can be clipped later.

When all four designs are filled in, sew rug binding to the burlap along the edge of the punched area. Then, turn the binding under and slip-stitch it to the back of each square, making sure the stitches do not show on the front of the rug. Miter the corners.

Join the squares to make a 48x48-inch rug, using an overcast stitch and carpet thread. Brush a layer of liquid latex onto the back of the rug, following the finishing directions on page 54.

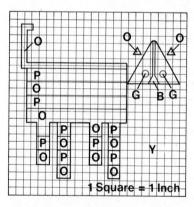

1 Square = 1 Inch

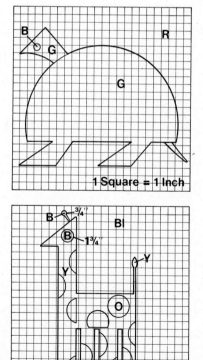

1 Square = 1 Inch

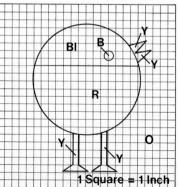

1 Square = 1 Inch

1 Square = 1 Inch

Design-Your-Own Scatter Rug and Pillow

Designing your own rug pattern is lots of fun and not at all difficult, as the small scatter rug and pillow pictured at the right illustrate. Just divide your rug fabric into four-unit blocks and create your own graceful pattern square-by-square. Or if you prefer, use our pattern below.

We worked this rug in earth-tone shades, but the design would be equally effective in six shades of another color, such as blue or green. Just select two light, two medium, and two dark shades of yarn.

Materials
Rug
28x40 inches heavy-duty burlap or punch-needle canvas

6 ounces each of Aunt Lydia's polyester rug yarn (or a similar substitute) in the following colors: #558 cream, #305 peach, #320 burnt orange, #325 rust, #420 brown, and #425 wood brown

Punch-needle tool

Rug frame or artist's stretcher strips

Waterproof marking pen

Liquid latex rug backing

Pillow
16x16 inches rug canvas

16x16 inches backing fabric

Pillow stuffing or 12-inch pillow form

1½ ounces each of Aunt Lydia's polyester rug yarn in the colors listed for rug (above)

Liquid latex

Directions
Rug
Begin by drawing a 2-inch margin around the rug backing with a waterproof marking pen, making a rectangle 24x36 inches. Divide the rectangle into six 12-inch squares. Then, using dotted lines, segment each square into four 6-inch squares. Draw a wavy line from the center of each of the 12-inch squares into all four corners, making a wavy "X" in each large square, and a wavy diagonal line across each of the smaller squares, as shown in the pillow at right. In the small squares, draw additional wavy lines on both sides of the center line, making stripes of varying widths, as shown in the pattern below. Note that there is a lot of variation in the direction and width of the "waves" in the squares that make up the design.

Or, following the directions on page 53, enlarge the pattern below and transfer it to each square of the fabric, rotating it to maintain the effect of the design.

Mount the backing in a frame for hooking. Set the punch-needle tool for ½-inch loops and hook the design, following the directions on page 38. Start by working three rows of loops along the lines dividing the small and large squares, using one of the dark shades (E). (Work one row right on the line, with the other rows on each side of the first one.) Then, punch-hook at least two rows of loops in the other dark shade (F) along the center line that runs diagonally across each small square (making the wavy "X" in the large square). Then, using the remaining four shades (A,B,C,D), work stripes across each block, varying the placement of colors and the width of the stripes from block to block. Punch loops close together, working about four loops per inch and about six rows per inch. Check the front of the rug occasionally to be sure pile is dense and rich-looking.

When all hooking is finished, remove the backing from the frame and finish the rug, following the directions on pages 54 and 55.

Pillow
Cut a 16-inch square of rug backing and draw a 12-inch square in the center. Divide the square into four smaller squares and mark the design, following the directions above for the rug. (Or, enlarge the pattern below and transfer it to the fabric.) Hook the design following the instructions above and on page 38.

To finish, coat the punched area with liquid latex. Sew the pillow front to back, stitching as close as possible to the punched area. Leave one side open. Turn, stuff, and slip-stitch the opening.

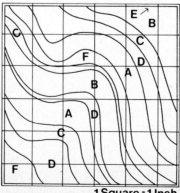

1 Square = 1 Inch

Color Key
A #558 Cream
B #305 Peach
C #320 Burnt Orange
D #325 Rust
E #420 Brown
F #425 Wood brown

Latch-Hooking: Earth-Toned Rug

To make this attractive circular rug, use a latch hook to knot the yarn into the backing fabric, with the cut ends on the front. The basic instructions help guide your steps.

Materials

68-inch circle #4 or #5 rug canvas (whichever is available and easiest for you to work with)

Washable rug yarn cut in 3-inch lengths, or precut rug yarn in 2½- to 3-inch lengths, depending on desired length of pile

Latch hook

Waterproof marking pen

Carpet thread

Rug binding

1 Square = 2 Inches

Directions

Enlarge the pattern below for the central motif, and transfer it to the center of the canvas, following the directions on page 53. Then add a 10-inch band (brown) around the center, two 1½-inch bands (gold and rust), and a final 3-inch band (green).

Referring to the photograph for colors, work the design following the general instructions for latch-hooking below.

Materials and Equipment

Latch-hooked rugs are worked on penelope canvas — a dual-thread, open-weave backing fabric. It is available in different sizes, designated according to the number of mesh, or spaces, per linear inch. You'll find rug canvas in #3½-, #4-, #5-, and #7-count sizes.

When purchasing canvas, add an extra 4 to 6 inches to the finished dimensions of the rug to allow for blocking and hemming. If you cannot purchase a single length large enough for the rug, piece together several sections. Overlap sections 2 inches, *matching warp and weft threads of both pieces.* (Warp threads are the straight grain of the fabric, parallel to the selvage.) Then, whipstitch sections together.

Bind edges of canvas with tape to keep them from unraveling or tearing yarn as you work.

Yarn for latch-hooked rugs is available precut in 2½- and 3-inch lengths, with 300 to 350 pieces per 1-ounce package. Or, use yarn from skeins cut to the length desired (usually 2 to 3 inches). Fold a 3 x 6-inch piece of cardboard in half lengthwise (into a "V"); wrap yarn around it. Then snip along the slot in the "V" with scissors, cutting yarn into pieces.

To determine the amount of yarn required, see page 59.

The latchet hook used to make the rug is a small tool with a hook at one end and a movable latchet bar beneath it. It pulls yarn into a lark's-head knot.

Making the Rug

Transfer design to canvas, following the directions on page 53. Make sure selvages of canvas are on the sides of the design rather than at top and bottom.

To work the design, lay the canvas right side up across a table and work from side to side and bottom to top, completing one row before moving to the next. Knot yarn into *weft* threads only, placing one knot in each square. As bottom rows become full, roll canvas into your lap.

To make each knot, grasp hook in one hand and wrap a piece of yarn around the shank, just below the latchet bar, keeping yarn ends even. Next, insert the hook into one space in the canvas and bring it out again in the space directly above, with the latchet bar open as shown in the diagram below. Then lay the ends of the yarn into the hook, as shown. Finally, pull the hook *back toward* you, out of the canvas. The latchet bar will close, making the knot.

Pull the ends of the yarn to tighten the knot. Continue, making knots across the row of canvas and changing colors whenever necessary.

Block and finish your rug, following directions on page 54.

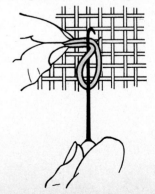

Contemporary Latch-Hooked Runner

Since this contemporary latch-hooked rug is assembled from 12-inch squares worked individually, you can make it any size you wish. After hooking a few squares, stitch them together to enjoy while you finish the others.

Or, work the rug into a 48 × 96-inch runner.

Materials
Thirty-two 16-inch squares of #5-count penelope rug canvas, or canvas pieced up to 52 × 100 inches (see note)
Acrylic rug yarn in bright primary colors (see note)
Latch hook
Waterproof marking pen
Brown wrapping paper
Carpet thread
Rug binding

Directions
Note: This rug is made of thirty-two 12-inch squares that can be worked one at a time and then sewn together. And while our rug measures 48 × 96 inches, you can make yours whatever size you wish simply by altering the number of squares or the way they are joined together. You can even make the rug entirely in one piece. To estimate yarn amounts, see page 59.

If you decide to make the rug in pieces, be sure to assemble the squares so that the large circle in the center of the design is evident (refer to the photograph to see how this is done).

Enlarge the pattern and transfer it to brown wrapping paper. To work the rug one square at a time, cut the rug canvas into 16-inch squares (this allows a 2-inch border of unworked canvas around all four sides) and center the squares on top of the pattern, one at a time. Trace each pattern onto canvas with a waterproof pen. To work the rug in one piece, transfer the designs to a single piece of canvas, leaving a 2-inch margin around the four outside edges.

Referring to the photograph for color ideas, outline each shape and fill it using a latch hook and acrylic rug yarn. (Refer to the latch-hook information on page 44 for basic how-to.) If you use skeins of rug yarn rather than precut pieces, cut the pieces into 2- or 3-inch lengths, depending on how long you want the pile.

To assemble the rug from squares, sew rug binding around each square; turn the 2-inch hem under and slip-stitch the binding to the back of the canvas. Piece the squares together with carpet thread so the rug measures four squares wide and eight squares long.

If you make the rug in one piece, sew binding to the four sides of the rug and turn the 2-inch margin under. Slip-stitch the binding to the back of the rug using carpet thread.

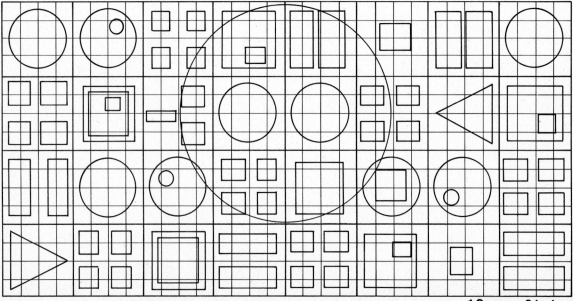

1 Square = 3 Inches

Quickpoint Stained-Glass Pattern

Stained-glass patterns are ideal for quickpoint designs as the spectacular rug at right proves. Because the backing can easily be divided into sections, your stitchery is readily portable–you can pack up your project and make the most of the moments set aside for rug making.

Use our tulip pattern, or stitch a rug from a stained-glass design of your own.

Materials
70-yard skeins Aunt Lydia's polyester rug yarn in the following amounts and colors: 4 #805 white, 6 #825 black, 4 #615 green, 1 #605 green, 2 #120 red, 2 #115 cerise, 2 #315 tangerine, and 2 #010 lilac
1½ yards #5-count 36-inch-wide rug canvas (or 2 yards if rug is worked in sections)
1½ yards 36-inch-wide black burlap
1 spool black carpet thread
Waterproof marking pen
Masking tape

Color Key
LG   Light green
DG   Dark green
O   Orange
PL   Purple
PK   Pink
W   White
R   Red
B   Black

Directions
This rug can be worked in one large piece or in three sections. If you work the rug as one piece, leave the canvas whole and bind the edges with masking tape. If you work the rug in sections, cut the canvas into three 21-inch pieces, making sure the warp threads, or lengthwise grain, runs the same direction on all three pieces. Bind all the edges with masking tape to keep the canvas from tearing the yarn or unraveling. The sections will be stitched together when the needlepoint is finished.

When working the rug in sections, divide the design at the black vertical lines. Make sure all three sections have the same number of stitches across so the pieces will match.

Enlarge the pattern below and transfer it to the canvas with a waterproof pen, following the directions on page 53. Begin by working the black lines, which are two stitches wide, in continental stitches. Then fill the colored areas in basket-weave stitches. (For stitch diagrams and how-to, see page 50.) As you stitch, try to keep tension even to avoid distorting the canvas.

To finish the rug, block the canvas as explained on pages 54 and 55. If the rug is worked in sections, backstitch the sections together, right sides facing, matching the design lines and the holes in the canvas. Use black carpet thread. Then fold side edges under and sew them to the back of the rug using a binding stitch.

Cut the remaining black yarn into 12-inch pieces and, using the rya knot shown on page 60, work a 5-inch fringe at both ends of the rug over two strands of canvas. Then turn canvas ends under; press, and slip-stitch to the back of the rug.

Place the rug face down and pin a piece of burlap to the back of the needlepoint, turning the edges of the burlap under as you pin. Sew the two layers together, using a slip stitch and black carpet thread and making sure no raw edges show.

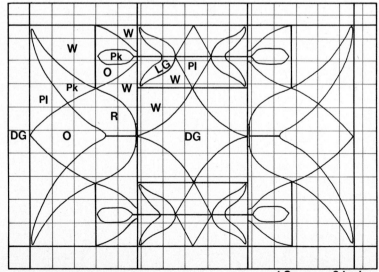

1 Square = 3 Inches

Quickpoint WELCOME Rug

*This traditional
WELCOME rug with its
Jacobean-style border
works up quickly and
easily on large-mesh
canvas. And it looks so
wonderfully inviting
mounted on the wall that
we've also included
directions for framing.
Patterns are on page 52.*

Materials

1⅓ yards 36-inch-wide
   #5-count interlock rug
   canvas
Wool rug yarn in the following
   colors and amounts: white
   (250 yards), dark blue (200
   yards), medium blue (50
   yards), and light blue (50
   yards)
Large tapestry needle
Masking tape
Waterproof marking pen
Graph paper
4 yards 1-inch-wide blue
   grosgrain ribbon (optional)
4 yards 4-inch-wide rug
   binding
11 feet 1 × 2-inch lumber
   (frame)
Wood glue and nails
Eye hooks and picture wire

Directions

Cut canvas 31 × 46 inches to allow a 2-inch margin around the design. Bind the edges of the canvas with masking tape to keep yarn from tearing on them. Then mark the center of the canvas with a waterproof pen by locating the middle horizontal and vertical threads.

The pattern shown on page 52 is for the upper left quadrant of the border design. Work from the chart, or copy the entire design onto graph paper by flopping the pattern to reproduce the stitch sequence for each quarter of the border.

Center the design on the canvas and begin by working the outermost dark blue border in continental stitches. Work the second and third blue borders, the floral motif, and the WELCOME letters in continental stitches. Fill the background in the center of the rug with white basket-weave stitches. (For an explanation of the stitches, see the diagrams below.)

Block the completed rug, following the directions on page 54.

To finish the rug, whip-stitch the edge of the rug binding securely to the edge of the needlepoint stitches around the edge of the rug. Assemble a 27 × 42-inch frame with the 1 × 2-inch lumber, glue, and nails. Then place the rug face down on a table and center the frame over it. Starting in the middle of each side, pull the margin of the rug to the back of the frame and staple in place. Miter the corners. The edge of the outermost blue border in the design should fall along the front of the frame.

For an attractive finish on the edge of the frame, blindstitch 1-inch-wide blue ribbon in place over the rug binding along the side edges of the frame. Attach eye hooks and picture wire for hanging.

continued

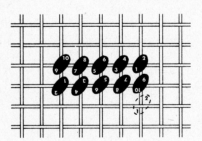

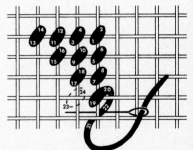

Continental stitch: Work from right to left on this stitch, turning the canvas on alternate rows as shown in the diagram. Bring the needle up at 1, down at 2, and up again a mesh ahead of the previous stitch (3). This makes a half-cross-stitch on the top and a slant stitch on the back. Keep tension uniform.

Basket-weave stitch: Begin in the upper right corner and work diagonally, moving the needle vertically on the down rows and horizontally on the up rows (see diagram). Increase one stitch on each side until you attain desired width. The sequence of stitches is indicated by the numbers shown on the diagram.

Quickpoint WELCOME Rug *(continued)*

center of
side border

(Actual dimen-
sions of rug are
42 X 27 inches
worked on five-
squares-per-inch
interlock canvas.
Pattern is ¼ of
border)

Color Key

⬧ Dark Blue
⊡ Medium Blue
◼ Light Blue

center of →
top border

1 Square = 1 Stitch

Enlarging and Transferring Designs

Enlarging (and Reducing) Designs

Patterns with grids — small squares laid over the design — are enlarged by drawing a grid of your own on paper, following the scale noted on the pattern. For example, if the scale is "1 square = 1 inch," you will need to draw a series of 1-inch squares on your paper to enlarge the drawing to the recommended size.

First, count the number of horizontal and vertical rows of squares on the original pattern. With a ruler, mark the exact same number of rows of larger squares on your paper. Number horizontal and vertical rows of squares in the margin of the original pattern. Then transfer numbers to corresponding rows on your pattern.

Begin by finding a square on your grid that corresponds with a square on the original.

Mark your grid wherever a design line intersects a line on the original grid. (Visually divide every line into fourths to gauge whether the design line cuts the grid line halfway or somewhere in between.)

Working one square at a time, mark each grid line where it is intersected by the design. After marking several squares, connect the marks with a continuous line following the contours of the original, as shown in the top and center diagrams at right.

Patterns without grids can be enlarged if you know any one of the dimensions of the final pattern. Draw a box around the design, making sure corners are square. Then draw a diagonal line between two opposite corners.

On the pattern paper, draw a right angle and extend the bottom line to the length of the new pattern. Lay the original in the corner and, using a ruler, extend the diagonal. Then draw a perpendicular line between the diagonal and the end of the bottom line, as in the lower diagram at right.

Divide the original and the new pattern into quarters and draw a second diagonal between corners. Number the sections, and transfer the design as explained in the directions above.

Transferring Designs

For punch-hooked rugs or any rug worked from the back of the fabric, remember that you must transfer a *mirror image of the pattern* to the back of the fabric so it will appear right side up on the face of the rug. So the first step is to make a tracing of the *back* of the enlarged pattern. Then transfer the pattern to the back of the burlap or other rug backing fabric in one of these two ways.

Use dressmaker's carbon paper and a tracing wheel or pencil, placing the carbon between fabric and pattern. Trace around design lines, using enough pressure to transfer them to the fabric.

Or, use a hot transfer pencil to trace the lines of the pattern. Then iron the transfer in place.

The final step is to go over outlines with a black waterproof pen so they are easy to see.

For latch-hooked rugs and other rugs to be worked on open-mesh canvas, enlarge the design onto paper and go over outlines with a waterproof pen to make them easily visible. Then tape the pattern to a large, flat surface. Center the canvas over it, with the canvas selvages along the sides of the pattern and the cut edges at the top and bottom; tape in place. The lines of the design should be visible through the holes in the canvas. Finally, with a waterproof pen, transfer the design outlines to the canvas.

When working with a pattern that needs to be enlarged or reduced and then transferred, choose the method that best suits your needs.

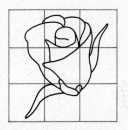

The original pattern

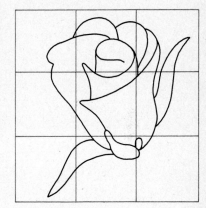

Enlarging on a grid

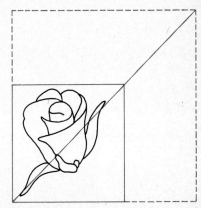

Enlarging without a grid

Finishing Techniques: Hooked and Needlepoint Rugs

Careful and expert finishing is the final step in crafting a beautiful handmade rug. Here are some techniques for backing, blocking, and hemming hooked and needlepoint rugs that will help you achieve a professional-looking result.

Finishing Punch-Hooked Rugs

Sealing the pile on a punch-hooked rug is essential to preserve its beauty. Otherwise, the loops will pull out, particularly if they've been clipped.

To secure the loops, you will need to coat the back of the rug with liquid latex rug backing — a strong but flexible rubber coating that binds the rug fibers to the fabric backing to hold them in place. It also helps to make the rug skid-proof.

There are two ways to back a punch-needle rug with latex, both of which are explained in the directions below.

One method of preparing a rug for the latex coating requires some tools and equipment: a board at least 2 to 3 inches larger all around than the finished rug (a piece of plywood works well), a hammer and nails, a carpenter's T-square or framing square, and a 1½- to 3-inch-wide paintbrush.

Remove the rug from the frame and lay it facedown on the board. Using the T-square or framing square, carefully align the corners of the rug, *so the lengthwise and crosswise threads of the backing fabric are at right angles to each other.* This is an extremely important step, for if the corners of the rug are not square when the latex is applied, the rug will be permanently distorted. Next, anchor the rug to the backing board with nails, spacing them 2 inches apart and 2 inches from the worked edge of the fabric.

An alternative method of finishing the rug is to apply latex to the back of the hooked area while it is on the rug frame. This is especially practical if the loops of the rug are long. To do this, make sure warp and weft threads of the fabric are at right angles. If they are not, adjust the backing fabric on the frame until

they are. Then coat the back of the loops with latex, following the directions below.

Following manufacturer's directions, use a paintbrush to apply liquid latex to the back of the *hooked area only.* If necessary, apply two thin coats of latex rather than one thick coat. Be careful not to paint latex onto unworked areas of the fabric.

Allow the latex to dry undisturbed for at least 24 hours. Then remove the nails from the fabric (or the fabric from the frame) and trim the unworked areas of the backing to within 3 inches of the hooked edge. If desired, add a fringe to the rug at this point by working two rows of rya knots into the margin along the hooked edge (see page 60 for directions).

To hem the rug, carefully apply a 2-inch-wide border of latex to the back of the rug around the hooked edge. Then double-fold the unworked margin and firmly press it into the latex with your fingers, sealing it to the back of the rug. If necessary, notch curved edges so they lie flat and smooth. Let the latex dry thoroughly — at least 24 hours; the rug is then ready to use.

Finishing Latch-Hooked and Needlepoint Rugs

Because latch-hooked and needlepoint rugs are frequently worked in your lap rather than on a frame, they may need to be straightened before they are hemmed. If your rug has lost its shape while being worked, you'll need to block it on a board that is 6 to 8 inches larger than the rug itself; a piece of plywood works well. You'll also need a carpenter's T-square or framing square, nails or staples, towels or other absorbent fabric, and a household sprayer or sprinkler bottle filled with water.

Cover the board with towels or

absorbent fabric and lay the rug facedown over them. Using a sprayer or sprinkler bottle, thoroughly moisten the back of the rug; do not get it soaking wet, however. Also, try not to get the margin on the canvas overly wet; it may pull apart.

Next, nail or staple to the board the margin of canvas along the top of the rug so that the rug edge is parallel to the edge of the board. Space nails and staples 2 inches apart and 1½ inches from the worked area of the canvas.

Pull the bottom edge of the rug into shape, using the T-square or framing square to check that lengthwise and crosswise threads are at right angles to each other. Pull the canvas taut and, starting in the center of the edge, nail or staple it to the board. Repeat the procedure for the sides of the rug, making sure the canvas is stretched taut and is square. Then let the rug dry thoroughly (for two to three days).

If the rug is worked in sections, block each section first, then stitch sections together, right sides facing, with backstiches along the worked areas of the canvas. Be sure to match the designs, and align the mesh of the adjoining sections carefully.

To make the rug skid-proof and to help prevent dirt from working into the underside, you may coat the back of the rug with liquid latex, following the directions above. Do this after the blocked rug is thoroughly dry, but before it is removed from the blocking board.

After blocking, the rug is ready for hemming.

To hem a latch-hooked or needlepoint rug, use 2-inch-wide cotton rug tape. For round or oval rugs, use bias tape. Sew tape around the rug along the canvas margin on the face of the design, stitching the edge of the tape as close to the worked edge of the rug as possible. Use strong thread, such as carpet thread, and small slip stitches or running stitches. Then trim the canvas underneath the rug tape to about ¾ inch.

Turn the rug over, wrong side up, and sew the tape to the back of the rug with overcast stitches or slip stitches. Ease the tape to the rug; do not pull tightly.

Miter the corners to avoid a bulky finish by first cutting a piece from the rug tape, as shown in the top diagram at right. Fold over one side of the tape and overcast-stitch it in place. Then fold over the other side, so the diagonal edges meet. Stitch the tape to the rug and then sew the two diagonal edges together, as shown in the lower diagram at right.

Lining a Rug

Occasionally a lining is called for in a handmade rug, usually to keep dirt away from the fibers in the rug. If you wish to add a lining to a rug made on canvas (punch-needle rugs do not need linings), select a firmly woven fabric in a color that compliments the colors used in the rug. Purchase fabric equal to the size of the rug plus an inch all around for the hem margin.

Block and hem the rug following the directions above. Then turn under a 1-inch hem on the lining fabric and blindstitch it to the edges of the rug with strong thread. Next, thread a needle with heavy thread that matches the background color in the rug and, working from the front, take tiny stitches through both the rug canvas and the lining. Knot the ends of the thread and clip them close to the knots so they will not show. Take only as many stitches as are needed to keep the lining smooth and even. Make sure the lining is secure.

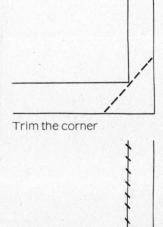

Trim the corner

Miter and stitch

Special Rug-Making Techniques

This enchanting rug is crocheted over a clothesline! And it's just one example of the exciting techniques for rug making you'll find in this section. Here also are a rya design and rugs to weave, appliqué, tie-dye, quilt, and "hook" on a sewing machine, as well as a section on personalizing purchased rugs. To learn to make the rug shown, please turn the page.

"Clothesline" Crochet *(shown on pages 56 and 57)*

What could be more fun than dressing up ordinary clothesline in brightly colored cotton yarns to make an attractive crocheted rug? And it's easy, too, for it's worked entirely in single-crochet stitches. The directions are for a 36x56-inch runner, but you can alter the dimensions just by changing the length of the beginning chain and the number of rows you stitch. Crochet abbreviations are on page 30, and the basic stitches are explained on page 34.

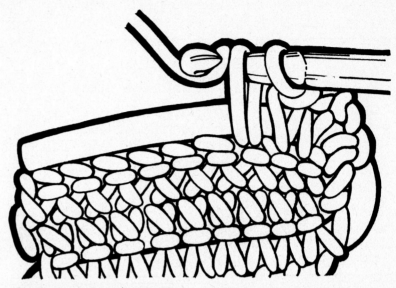

Single crochet over clothesline

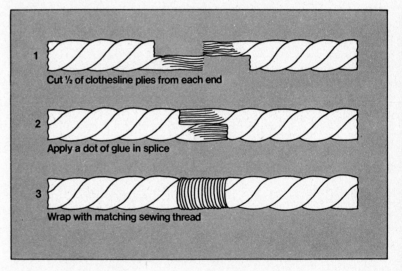

1 Cut ½ of clothesline plies from each end

2 Apply a dot of glue in splice

3 Wrap with matching sewing thread

Materials
Three 80-yard skeins Aunt Lydia's cotton rug yarn in each of the following colors: red, orange, yellow, light green, dark green, blue, and purple
50 yards clothesline
Size I crochet hook

Directions
With red yarn, ch 101.

Row 1: Sc in second ch from hook, and in each ch across — 100 sc — ch 2, turn.

Row 2: Hold end of clothesline next to rug, and sc around clothesline in each sc across, following the diagram above. Ch 1, turn.

Row 3: Sc in each st across — 100 sc. Change to orange (crocheting over yarn ends) and repeat these three rows in the following sequence: yellow, light green, dark green, blue, and purple. Repeat these 21 rows six times more, or for length desired; fasten off.

If necessary, splice clothesline by unraveling 1½ inches on end of each piece. Cut out half the ply of each piece, and overlap. Secure with dot of glue and wrap splice with matching color of sewing thread, as shown above.

How to Estimate Materials Requirements for a Rug

For hooked, needlepoint, and rya rugs, the first step in estimating materials needed for a design is to determine as closely as possible the total number of square inches of each color in the pattern. The easiest way to do this is to enlarge the pattern onto paper marked into one-inch squares, following directions on page 53 for enlarging on a grid.

Next, mark each color area, inch by inch, throughout the design. When a color fills only part of a square, estimate what fraction of an inch that color requires. Finally, total the number of square inches in each color; make a note of the amount.

The second step is to determine the amount of material required to work one square inch of the design in the technique and materials you've selected for your project. Purchase a small amount of each of the materials you intend to use, such as yarn and backing fabric. Then work a sample swatch in the technique you've chosen, following the specific directions below.

Finally, multiply the amount of material needed to work one square inch by the total number of square inches of each color in the design to determine the number of yards or pieces of material required. Then, just to be on the safe side, add a little extra to allow for waste, unless you've already been generous in your yarn estimates.

Punch-Hooked and Needlepoint Rugs

Purchase a small piece of backing fabric and hook or stitch a one-inch square with the needle and yarn you intend to use in the rug. For a punch-hooked rug, determine the length of the loops best suited to the design, and the correct spacing between loops for the best coverage of the fabric (so no backing shows).

Determine the amount of yarn needed to cover one square inch by carefully pulling out the yarn in the finished sample. Measure the length of the yarn (in yards), then compute requirements, following directions above.

Latch-Hooked Rugs

A package of precut yarn, containing 300 to 350 pieces, will cover the number of square inches of canvas shown below:

Canvas Size	300 Pieces	350 Pieces
3½-count	24½	28½
4-count	18¾	22
5-count	12	14
7-count	6	4

To latch-hook a rug with yarn in skeins, determine the number of yards per skein, the length you intend to cut pieces for hooking, and the number of pieces that can be cut from each skein. Referring to the chart above, compute the amount required. For example, with 70-yard skeins cut into 3-inch lengths, you'll get 840 pieces from each skein, and these will cover 52½ square inches of #4-count rug canvas.

Rya Rugs

Transfer the design to rya backing fabric first. Then, compute the number of knots either by counting the knotting spaces or by estimating the number of square inches in each color area.

Work a sample square inch of knots, threading the needle with the number of strands of yarn you intend to use and making loops the desired length. As you stitch, keep track of the amount of yarn used. Compute final requirements by multiplying the amount required for one knot (or square inch of knots) by the total number of knots (or square inches) in that color and yarn.

If you've found a rug design that you'd like to work in a different technique or material than that called for in the directions, or if you've designed your own pattern, you'll need to estimate the amount of yarn or other materials needed to complete your project.

Here are some tips to guide you in determining these requirements for hooked, needlepoint, and rya rugs. To estimate requirements for rag and braided rugs, see page 6; for woven rugs, turn to page 87.

Dramatic Rya Rug

*Beautiful pile rugs can be
made with a needle as
well as a hook. And by
threading the needle with
several yarns in two or
three colors, and by
varying the length of the
pile from section to
section in the design, you
can achieve the exciting
results seen opposite in
our 32 × 50-inch rya rug.*

Materials

36 × 54 inches rya rug backing
    fabric
65-yard skeins of Marks
    (Swedish) rya rug yarn or a
    suitable substitute in the
    following amounts and
    colors: 2 #1912 rust, 2 #1911
    rust, 1 #1983 blue, 1 #1993
    blue, 2 #1933 brown, 13
    #1934 brown, 4 #92 black, 5
    #1953 white, 5 #1901 ivory,
    5 #91 ecru
Two 150-yard skeins each of
    Marks (Swedish)
    tapestry-weight rya rug yarn
    in #644 orange and #536
    orange, or a suitable
    substitute
Four to twelve 2¾-inch blunt,
    heavy rug needles
Waterproof marking pen
Carpet thread
Masking tape

Directions

Enlarge the pattern opposite and transfer it to the fabric with a waterproof pen, following the directions on page 53. The long sides of the
design should parallel the selvages of the fabric. Leave a 2-inch
margin along each edge; bind raw edges with masking tape. To work
the design, turn the fabric sideways with selvages on the sides and cut
edges at the top and bottom.

   Stitch the design in rya knots, working from left to right across the
fabric and from the lower edge to the top. Position knots in the open
spaces that fall approximately every ½ inch along the length of the
fabric. Work each row all the way across the fabric before moving on
to the next one.

   To make each knot, thread the needle with the number of strands of
yarn indicated below. Insert the needle at A, as shown in the diagram
at left, below. Bring it up at B, carry it across the warp threads, and
bring it down at C. Bring it up again at A. Pull the yarn to tighten the
knot. To keep loops uniform, wrap yarn around a piece of cardboard
cut to size when making each knot, as shown in the diagram at right,
below. When each row is complete, clip loops.

   For section 1, thread one needle with two shades of dark brown,
one with dark brown and black, and the third with dark brown and
light brown. Work 2-inch loops and mix colors by changing needles.
For section 2, thread a needle with one strand each of white, ivory,
and ecru. Work 1-inch loops.

   For section 3, thread one needle with two shades of rust; work
2-inch loops. For section 4, work 2-inch loops using two needles
—one threaded with two strands of dark brown and the other
threaded with dark brown and black. Alternate needles as you stitch.

   For section 5, work 2-inch loops. Outline the circle primarily in
blue-green, mixing in a few royal blue knots. For the center, use three
strands of white as in section 2. Skip every fourth stitch to allow for
the extra weight of the third strand. Use 5 strands of orange yarn,
alternating the two different shades, to make lines inside the circle, as
shown in the photograph.

   To finish the rug, remove the masking tape and turn under the
edges 1 inch. Turn them under again, miter the corners, and pin in
place. Whipstitch the edges to the back of the rug with carpet thread.
To hang the rug, stitch metal curtain rings along upper back.

Making a rya knot

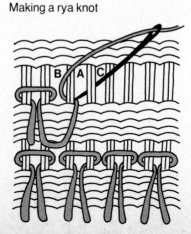

Making uniform loops

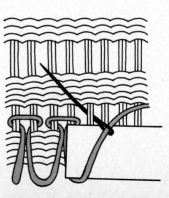

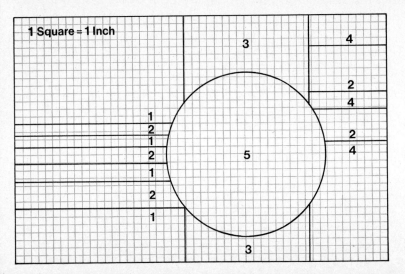

1 Square = 1 Inch

Weaving with Fabric Strips

All your scraps from spring sewing can be used to craft our refreshing-as-ice-cream rug, opposite. It's made with cotton fabrics cut into slim strips and woven into broad and narrow bands over cotton or linen carpet warp. Directions include how-to instructions for building your own frame loom just for this 3 x 5-foot rug.

Materials

Two pieces lumber, 2x4x48 inches
Two pieces lumber, 2x4x60 inches
Four angle irons
Screws
Cotton gingham, plaid, print, and solid-color fabrics in pink, yellow, and green equal to about 15 yards of 44/45-inch-wide fabric (see note)
Large-eyed tapestry needle or weaver's shuttle
800 yards cotton carpet warp

Directions

Note: This rug can be made from sewing scraps, remnants, used clothing, or new yardage. For best results, use prints that are woven into the fabric rather than printed on it. One yard of 44/45-inch-wide fabric yields 24 strips.

When using old clothing, prepare it for cutting, following the directions on pages 6 and 7. Then cut fabric into 1½-inch-wide strips using the shortcut method (see page 20). Roll strips into balls. When you are ready to weave a ball of strips, fold raw edges of strips to the inside. Then fold strip in half lengthwise, as shown on page 6, to hide raw edges.

While this rug may be made on a regular loom, you may also make it on a box loom that you build yourself. To construct a loom for the rug, build a 48x60-inch box frame from the 2x4s, butting the corners and securing them with angle irons and screws. Then, measure in 6 inches from each end to mark the central 36 inches on each short side of the loom.

To warp the loom, tie one end of the linen warp securely to the 2x4 at one of the 6-inch marks. Carry the linen cord up to the top of the frame, around it, and across to the opposite side of the frame. Wrap it around the frame, carry it across again, and wrap it around the 2x4 again next to the first warp. Wrap in a figure-eight (when viewed from the side). Continue in this way until you've wrapped the frame 200 times, creating 400 warp threads in the 36-inch space. Pull the warp thread tightly as you wrap around the frame. Knot the ends of the warp string together when necessary; fabric weft will cover the knots. Firmly knot the end of the last warp to the frame.

To begin the rug, first weave with the warp thread to a depth of ½ inch. On the first row, go over and under *4 threads at a time to establish 100 multiple-thread warps in the rug.* On the second row, go over the threads you went under on the first row and under those you went over. Repeat these two rows for the remainder of the rug. Keep warps evenly spaced as you weave (¼ to ⅜ inch apart). As you weave each row, beat it down firmly against the previous rows by pushing with your fingers to make the weaving snug and firm so there are no gaps between the rows.

To weave with fabric strips, thread the end of a fabric strip into a needle or weaving shuttle and weave over and under 4 threads across the warp. Begin and end lengths of fabric within the warp rather than at the outer edges so the sides of the rug will be stable. Keep outer warps straight as you weave. Weave fabric in bands of color between 2 and 6 inches wide, as shown in the photograph.

At the upper end of the rug, after weaving the last row of fabric strips, weave a ½-inch-wide band of carpet warp again, to match the ½ inch woven at the beginning of the rug.

To remove the rug from the box loom, carefully cut the warp threads and knot as follows. Cut the first two multiple-strand warps off the loom. Tie together the four strands in the outside warp and *two strands* from the adjoining warp in an overhand knot. Leave ends long for the fringe. Then cut the next multiple-strand warp from the loom and tie together two strands from that warp with the two remaining from the previous warp. Continue cutting and tying together strands from adjoining warps until the rug is completely off the loom. Trim ends of warp threads evenly so the fringe is between three and five inches long.

Off-Loom Weaving

Card weaving is an easy and exciting technique for making strips to stitch into rugs. To make your own cards, cut twenty-two 3½-inch cardboard squares and punch holes in each card one inch diagonally from each corner. Then mark cards with letters as shown below, warp them, and weave this sturdy 24x36-inch rug.

Materials
70-yard skeins Aunt Lydia's polyester rug yarn (or a suitable substitute) in the following amounts and colors: 18 #825 black, 4 #145 brick, and 12 #565 antique gold
22 four-hole weaving cards
Heavy-duty thread

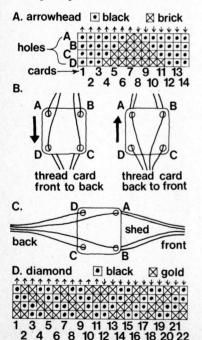

A. arrowhead   ⊡ black   ⊠ brick
holes { A B C D
cards → 1 3 5 7 9 11 13
        2 4 6 8 10 12 14

B.
A B   A B
D C   D C
thread card   thread card
front to back   back to front

C.
      D   A
back   shed   front
      C   B

D. diamond   ⊡ black   ⊠ gold
1 3 5 7 9 11 13 15 17 19 21
2 4 6 8 10 12 14 16 18 20 22

Directions
Start with arrowhead strips. Cut eighteen 5-yard pieces of black yarn and ten 5-yard pieces of brick for warp threads. Tie together all the warp threads in a tight bundle at the center, using one yard of scrap yarn. Anchor the ends of the tie to a doorknob or table leg and spread ends of the warp threads in front of you.

To thread cards for weaving, number 14 cards from 1 to 14. To thread, hold each card at an angle to your body with lettered side facing left. Each hole will be threaded with one strand of yarn. Study diagram A for colors; arrows at the top of the diagram indicate threading direction (up or down). Diagram B indicates how to thread the card in each direction. If the arrow in diagram A points up, thread the card from right (back) to left (front). If the arrow points down, thread from left (front) to right (back).

Following diagram A, begin threading with card 1. Since the arrow is going up, thread each strand of black yarn from the back of the card through to the front. Then pull the yarn strands through the holes about 12 inches beyond the card. Repeat for card 2; then stack 2 atop 1. Continue threading and stacking cards according to the colors and arrows in diagram A. Note that cards 1 to 7 are threaded in one direction (up), while cards 8 to 14 are threaded in the opposite direction (down).

After threading cards, tie a cord around them. There should be 12 inches of yarn in front of the cards; the rest should be in back.

Gather the free ends of the warp in one hand. With the other end of the yarn still fastened to the table leg, pull the free ends until they are taut. Then knot the free ends together tightly with a piece of yarn. Secure this end (the front in diagram C) to your waist around a belt or belt loop. Sit far enough from the table leg so the warp threads remain taut at all times.

To weave, wind four strands of black yarn around a shuttle or into a ball. Hold the pack of cards upright, as shown in diagram C. Draw black weft yarns through the shed (shown in diagram C) between the cards and your body, leaving the first 6 inches of the yarn ball free to weave into the strip when the weaving is complete. Holding the cards as a unit, turn them *forward* to create a new shed. (You started with holes AD on top and, after turning, holes BA will be on top.) Draw the weft through that shed.

If some cards don't turn, make sure they're threaded properly. After each row (one turn of the cards), beat back the weft threads tightly, pushing them toward your body. Also stop periodically to untwist the warp yarns beyond the cards. Continue turning cards in the same forward direction, passing the weft through each new shed until the woven strip is 36 inches long. Then untie the knots and remove the cards, but don't trim the fringe yet. Make three more arrowhead strips in the same way.

For the diamond design, cut twenty-two 5-yard pieces each of black and gold yarn. Thread all cards following diagram D. Prepare warp threads, following directions above. Use black for weft.

To weave, work 14 rows, turning the cards *forward* as you did with the arrowhead strips. Work the next 14 rows, turning the cards *backward*, in the opposite direction. Continue until weaving measures 36 inches. Weave six strips.

To assemble the rug, stitch strips together with heavy-duty thread, using the photograph as a guide. Trim ends of fringe evenly.

Felt Appliqué

Our handsome reproduction of a 100-year-old Navaho rug, shown opposite, is fabulously fast and easy to make in felt appliqué. You need only cut out the pieces, layer them atop one another on a backing fabric, and stitch them together to make this 54 × 62-inch rug. Then display it on the floor or finish it for hanging as we did.

Materials

Note: All requirements are based on 72-inch-wide felt
1²/₃ yards white felt
1¹/₃ yards black felt
1 yard purple felt
2 yards red felt
1¹/₃ yards green felt
1¼ × 62-inch lath strip
52 × 63-inch piece of lining material
Picture hangers
White glue

Directions

Cut white felt 57½ × 63 inches for the background. From black felt, cut one 8 × 63-inch strip, one 5½ × 63-inch strip, one 12 × 63-inch strip, and four 3¼ × 63-inch strips. Stitch the 8-inch strip to the top of the background and the 5½-inch strip to the bottom, making sure edges are flush. Sew the 12-inch strip to the middle of the background. (To find the central 12 inches, measure 30 inches down from the top; mark this point. Then measure 6 inches up and 6 inches down from the mark.) In the white areas above and below the center black strip, evenly space and sew 3¼-inch black strips—two to the top and two to the bottom.

Cut and stitch two 1¼ × 63-inch green strips to bottom black strip (evenly spaced), as shown opposite. Repeat for top black strip.

Following the diagram below, cut the center cross from purple felt, making the two side bars 27 inches long. Cut four 1¼ × 20½-inch green strips and two 1¼ × 20½-inch black strips, and stitch to sides of cross as shown — green on top and bottom and black in the middle, with purple between.

To cut the red and green center crosses, cut a 14 × 19½-inch red piece and an 11½ × 17-inch green one. Cut a 5 × 6½-inch piece from each corner of both rectangles. Center and stitch the green cross over the red one; then center and stitch the red one over the purple one. Stitch the entire purple cross to the center black strip.

Referring to the outer cross pattern, cut fabric as follows: cut four 22 × 23-inch red rectangles, four 19½ × 21-inch green rectangles, four 17 × 18½-inch purple rectangles, and four 14½ × 16-inch red rectangles. Next, cut 4½ × 5½-inch rectangles from all corners of large rectangles. (The 5½-inch side is the length and the 4½-inch side is the width.) Layer the pieces according to size and stitch. Position one cross in each corner of the background and stitch.

Cut the diamond motif strips from 1¾-inch-wide strips of felt folded lengthwise. Mark each strip at even intervals and cut triangles between each interval. Make these strips any length, intermingling both black and white. For the center cross, repeat the procedure using ⁷/₈-inch-wide strips.

Sew the lining to the background piece, right sides together, in a ½-inch seam. Leave an opening for turning. Turn and slip-stitch opening. Turn 2½ inches under along the top to make a casing for the lath strip or dowel. Insert the strip and attach picture hangers according to package directions.

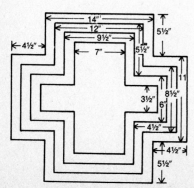

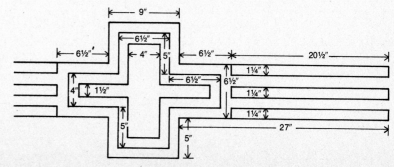

Canvas Floor Cloths:
Padded Exercise Mats

Canvas is a wonderful fabric for floors because it's heavy, strong, and long-wearing. And when quilted, it makes a practical and comfortable exercise mat like the one shown below.

When sewing on canvas, use a heavy needle and thread and stitch slowly to avoid breaking the sewing machine needle.

Materials
3¼ yards 52-inch-wide unprimed natural artist's canvas
90x108 inches quilt batting
Thread to match canvas

Directions
Pre-shrink canvas by washing in warm water. Iron while still slightly damp. Cut one 37x55-inch piece of canvas and one 36x54-inch piece. Also cut four 36x54-inch pieces of quilt batting.

To make the cover for the mat, baste a ½-inch hem around all four sides of the 37x55-inch piece of canvas. Then stack the pieces of quilt batting atop one another on the floor and lay the basted piece of canvas, right side up, over them. Pin all layers securely together, starting in the center and working toward the edges. Space pins 4 to 6 inches apart.

Turn the pinned canvas and batting over so the batting side is up. Lay the remaining piece of canvas on top and pin in place. Turn the basted edges of the lower piece of canvas ½ inch over the raw edges of the upper piece, covering all raw edges of canvas and batting. Using thread to match fabric, machine-stitch along the fold on all four sides, making sure that you sew through all layers. Remove pins and smooth out the fabric layers.

To finish, mark and stitch nine 4-inch "tubes" down the length of the mat, making sure your lines are straight.

Tie-Dyed Rug

Directions

Hem the two ends of the canvas and wash to remove any sizing. Starting in the middle, gather the canvas into cones; tie each cone at various levels with polished cotton twine, as shown in the diagram at right. Tying at different levels up and down the cones will vary the width of each band of color. Tie the cones *tightly* to prevent dye penetration under the twine and beyond the area to be dyed.

Tie cones up and down the canvas, placing them as desired. The more cones, the more color, since each cone is dipped in dye. If you use more than one color dye, be sure to keep them in separate containers so the colors don't mix. To speed dyeing, add ¼ teaspoon of water softener to each pint of water. Also, wet the canvas before dyeing to help it absorb dye more evenly.

Prepare the fabric dye according to directions, and test it with fabric scraps before dyeing the canvas. Dip each tied section into the dye, letting the dye absorb into the cones. (When the dye is exhausted the colors will begin to look pale.) Rinse each cone in cold water and untie the twine. Rinse the cones again until the water runs clear. Let canvas dry flat; steam-press when dry.

For a uniquely dramatic rug, tie-dye a length of canvas for your floor. First wash canvas in hot water to remove the sizing, then tie sections into knots and dip them into dye for the stunning sunburst effect shown below.

Materials
36x128-inch piece of
  heavy-weight natural canvas
Polished cotton twine
Brownish rust fabric dye (or
  color of your choice)

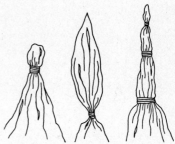

Tying cones for dyeing

Sewing Machine "Hooking": A Quick-and-Easy Rug

"Hook" a rug on a sewing machine? It's easy! Our luxurious 3x5-foot throw, opposite, is made by wrapping rug yarn around a hairpin lace frame, then stitching down the frame's center with nylon thread to form long strips. Position these strips on a fabric backing and stitch them down the center a second time. Then either cut the yarn or leave it looped.

Materials

Sewing machine
Ten 2-ounce skeins white rug yarn
Eight 2-ounce skeins yellow rug yarn
2½-inch-wide hairpin lace frame (available in needlecraft shops)
4-inch-wide hairpin lace frame
Clear nylon thread for spool
White thread for bobbin
1¾ yards washable duck canvas or rug burlap
Liquid latex rug backing
Tissue paper

Directions

Cut rug backing 40 x 64 inches. Draw a 2-inch border around the rug for the hem, and a second border, 6 inches wide, inside the first one for the yellow yarn.

To make white rug yarn loops, use the 2½-inch lace frame. With the curved part close to you, begin wrapping rug yarn around the frame, keeping the loops close together as you wind (as shown in the left diagram below).

Thread the sewing machine with clear nylon thread on top and white thread in the bobbin. Lower the feed dogs. When several inches of yarn loops have been wrapped, stitch the yarn down through the *middle* of the lace frame. Be sure to keep the yarn loops close together without gaps. As the yarn is stitched, let it slide off the open end of the frame; pull the frame toward you, and continue wrapping the yarn around the frame. When you've made a strip of yarn loops 48 inches long, cut the yarn and begin a new strip. Make 27 white yarn strips and 8 yellow yarn strips, each 48 inches long. Also stitch eight 36-inch yellow strips.

Place a large piece of tissue paper or lightweight interfacing *under* the rug canvas to prevent puckering as you stitch. (It tears off easily when you have finished stitching.)

The completed rectangular rug consists of 27 rows of white yarn strips in the center surrounded by 4 rows of yellow strips along each side for a border. To stitch the yarn strips in place, position a long yellow strip along the edge of one side of the backing and parallel to the center panel. Stitch down the center of the yarn strip a *second* time, to secure it to the backing (see the how-to photograph below). For the second row of yellow strips, hold the first row out of the way and stitch the second one alongside. Its center seam will be 1 to 1½ inches from the seam on the first row of yellow loops. Sew a third and fourth row of yellow loops to the backing inside the 6-inch border. Then stitch rows of white loops, spacing center seams only ¼ inch apart. This gives the rug a plush look and hides the backing fabric. Continue stitching strips to the backing until the rug is complete.

Clip the yellow yarn loops with scissors when the rug is finished. Do not cut the white yarn loops.

Turn the 2-inch hem to the back of the rug and press; slip-stitch the hem to the rug back. Apply liquid latex to the back, if desired. Do not use the rug in high-traffic areas.

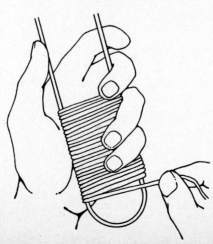

Sewing Machine "Hooking" *(continued)*:
Floral Throw Rug

Directions

Note: The finished size of this rug is approximately 26 x 44 inches. Dimensions below allow for a 2-inch hem.

Enlarge the patterns below and transfer motifs to a 48x30-inch oval of backing fabric using dressmaker's carbon paper. Follow the oval drawing for proper placement of the rug motifs.

Place a large sheet of tissue paper *under* the fabric backing to help prevent puckering as you sew.

Thread the sewing machine with clear nylon thread to hide the stitches. Then remove the machine's presser foot and lower the feed dogs. Beginning with the design areas and following the color key, stitch loops of yarn to the canvas backing. It is easiest to stitch one area of color at a time.

To attach yarn loops, first stitch the end of a length of yarn to the material. Pull up a yarn loop using the knitting needle or pencil to the *right* of the sewing machine needle, as shown in the inset photograph at left, opposite. Stitch slowly over the base of the yarn loop to secure it to the backing. Then pull up the next loop alongside the first one and stitch it in place. Continue pulling and stitching loops in this manner to complete each color area, as shown in the right inset photograph. Change yarn color when necessary. Be sure to place the loops close enough that no backing fabric shows through.

To fill in the ivory background areas faster, use several lengths of yarn together and pull up more than one loop at a time. Then, stitch across all loop bases at the same time.

When the rug is complete, turn the 2-inch fabric margin to the back of the rug and press. Slip-stitch the margin in place, trimming excess to eliminate bulk. Apply a nonskid backing of liquid latex, if desired.

(Note: Although this rug is sturdy, it is not designed for high-traffic areas. Clean the rug by dry cleaning it.)

You can "hook" this traditional design on your sewing machine with beautiful results. Our splashy floral rug looks hooked, but is actually worked entirely of closely spaced loops of rug yarn stitched in place by machine.

Materials

- 1⅓ yards washable duck canvas or rug burlap for backing
- Three 2-ounce skeins ivory rug yarn
- ½ skein rug yarn in each of the following colors: yellow, gold, rust, plum, olive green, and dark green
- Knitting needle, pencil, or other instrument for lifting yarn loops
- Clear nylon thread for spool
- White thread for bobbin
- Tissue paper
- Dressmaker's carbon paper
- Liquid latex rug backing

Color Key

- D Dark green
- O Olive green
- P Plum
- G Gold
- R Rust
- Y Yellow

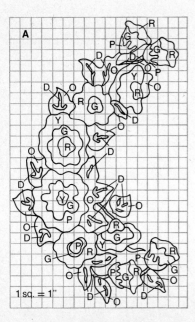

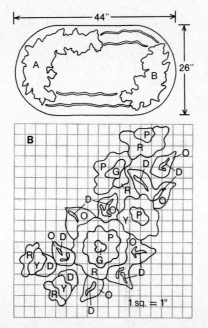

Personalizing Purchased Rugs:
Embroidered Rug

Sometimes, just one little touch can make all the difference between a so-so room and one that's extra special. Here we plucked a motif from the luxurious sheets and comforter, then embroidered a simplified version on an everyday area rug. The result? A coordinated bedroom with a "custom-made" embroidered rug.

Materials
8x10-foot rug with an uncut pile
Heavy rug yarn in appropriate colors
Approximately 8 yards 1-inch-wide white nylon braid
Large-eyed tapestry needle

Directions
Select a motif you would like to duplicate. In this case, we chose the floral-and-lattice design on the sheets, but since it was too small and intricate to reproduce on the rug, we simplified and enlarged it. If necessary, use tracing paper to copy a motif from your sheets. See directions on page 53 for enlarging designs.

Leaving a 12-inch border around the rug, appliqué white braid in a lattice-like pattern to the rug.

Using simple stitches like satin, stem, and chain stitches and French knots, embroider the flowers on and around the lattice. Repeat the motif in each corner, varying the position of the flowers.

If the pile is too thick to embroider directly on the rug, work the embroidery on felt, cut out the felt pieces, and appliqué them to the rug with heavy thread.

It's best to use wool yarn on a wool rug and synthetic yarn on a synthetic rug.

Coat the embroidery with soil repellent to help keep it clean.

Personalizing Purchased Rugs *(continued):*
A Sunburst Rug from Remnants

Want a one-of-a-kind rug at a bargain-basement price? If so, turn to carpet remnants. Just three small pieces of broadloom artfully pieced together make this sunburst design. When choosing remnants for a rug such as this, select pieces with pile all about the same height.

Materials
Broadloom carpet (12 feet wide) in the following lengths and colors: 2 feet blue, 1½ feet yellow, and 1¼ feet green
Utility knife
Brown wrapping paper
Waterproof marking pen
60-inch circle heavy-duty burlap
Double-faced carpet tape

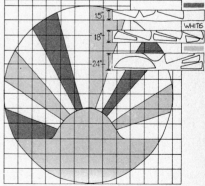

1 Square = 6 Inches

Directions
Note: The finished rug is about five feet in diameter.

Enlarge the pattern at right on brown paper, following directions on page 53. Number the sun's rays on the pattern from 1 to 12 and note the color of each ray. Then cut the pattern apart and use the individual sections as patterns for cutting the carpet.

Lay the broadloom remnants on the floor, wrong side up, and then lay the pattern pieces in position as shown in the diagram at right. Be sure to position the two pattern pieces in the sun section so the pile direction is the same on both pieces. Trace around each piece with a waterproof marking pen and mark the number of the ray on the back of the carpet.

Using a sharp utility knife and working from the wrong side of each remnant, cut out individual pieces.

Using double-faced carpet tape (sticky on both sides), bind the individual pieces of carpet to the burlap backing fabric. Anchor the sun section first, then the rays in numerical order.

Personalizing Purchased Rugs *(continued):*

Needlepoint Borders

Our 12-inch quickpoint border adds personal pizzazz to a carpet remnant. To make it, work strips of canvas in simple basket-weave and continental stitches. Then join strips together, work the corners, and stitch the borders to a 30x42-inch piece of carpet.

Materials
30x42 inches beige carpeting (purchased)
6¼x4 feet of #5-count canvas
70-yard skeins acrylic rug yarn in the following amounts and colors: 12 white, 8 blue, and 6 brown
Carpet thread
7 yards carpet tape
Large-eyed tapestry needle
Heavy-duty sewing needle

Color Key
☐ brown (3 stitches)
■ blue (9 stitches)
☐ white

Directions
Note: The finished size of the rug is 54x66 inches.

Cut two 70x16-inch strips of canvas and two 34x16-inch strips of canvas. These measurements allow for 2-inch margins of unworked canvas. Bind the raw edges of the canvas with masking tape. Mark the center horizontal and vertical threads on each canvas strip.

Begin the quickpoint pattern in the middle of a 70-inch strip. Starting with brown yarn, work the design following the pattern below. Stop within 14 inches of both ends. Then, work the blue yarn and fill in the background with white yarn, again stopping within 14 inches of the ends. Repeat for the second 70-inch strip, making sure the stitches are worked in the same direction.

Join one of the 34-inch strips to one of the already-worked 70-inch strips by overlapping the top left-hand edge of the 70-inch strip over the bottom two inches of the short side of the 34-inch strip. Line up outside edges to make a right angle. Match the holes and whipstitch the two pieces together. Work the corner, following the pattern and stitching through both pieces of canvas where the strips overlap, keeping the holes aligned.

Work up the left-hand side of the rug to within five inches of the end of the strip. Repeat overlapping procedure on right-hand side and continue working the design as for the left-hand side.

Lay the second 70-inch strip across the top ends of the two short strips, matching corners, holes, and pattern lines. Trim excess canvas if necessary, and whipstitch the strips together where they overlap. Complete stitching on remaining corners, working through two layers of canvas where the pieces overlap.

Block the finished border, following the instructions on page 54. Fold under and press 2-inch margins of unworked canvas along the outside edge of the border. Whipstitch the edges of the back of the border and mask with carpet tape.

Cut a 30x42-inch piece of purchased carpet and whipstitch it to the inside 2-inch margins.

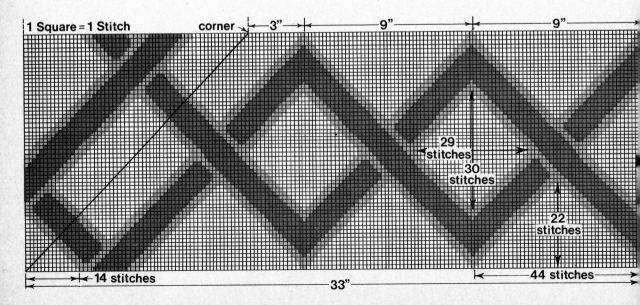

1 Square = 1 Stitch   corner   3"   9"   9"
29 stitches   30 stitches   22 stitches
14 stitches   33"   44 stitches

Creative Rug Making

Yes, you can macrame a rug, as our unique rope runner proves! It's simply a matter of turning your talents in new directions. And in this section, you'll find other exciting and unusual rugs to stimulate your creativity. For example, you can think big and weave a stack of small rugs to join into a stairway runner, or think small and stitch a miniature. You can show off your mastery of many techniques in a single rug, or use just one technique—speed hooking—to work a rug in a hurry. Directions for the runner begin on the next page.

Macrame Rug *(shown on pages 78 and 79)*

The attractive runner shown on pages 78 and 79 features stylized animals and a central Tree of Life design worked with double half-hitch knots in Cavandoli stitches. Separating the panels are bands of alternating square knots. Patterns for the panels are on pages 82 and 83.

Materials
2-ply jute in the following colors and amounts: 1500 yards natural, 150 yards dark red, 150 yards brown, 150 yards dark green, 150 yards rust, and 150 yards dark blue
18x36 inches of ⅜-inch plywood
Heavy-duty sewing needle
Dental floss or carpet thread
Fast-drying craft glue
Liquid latex rug backing
Staple gun and staples

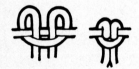

Lark's head knot

Square knot

Directions
Note: The finished size of the runner shown on pages 78 and 79 is 22x68 inches. To make it wider, increase the numbers of knots in multiples of 14, since each animal block is 14 knots wide. (Each block of 14 knots is approximately 2¾ inches wide.) To make the runner longer, increase the depth of the border design or of the alternating square-knot panels. You'll also need to alter the amounts of cord needed for the runner if you increase the size.

To make the rug in the size shown, cut a 36-inch bearer cord from natural jute; then, cut fifty-six 4-yard lengths of natural jute. Fold the 56 pieces in half and attach each one to the bearer cord with a lark's head knot, as shown in the top diagram at left. Staple the bearer cord to the top of the plywood board along the 36-inch side, making sure the ends of the cords are free for tying.

To work the border at the top of the runner, staple a piece of brown jute about 2 yards long to the left side of the plywood so it is perpendicular to the cords at the point where the border design is to begin (just below the lark's head knots). Following the border diagram on page 83, work six rows in Cavandoli stitches, which are explained on page 82. Note that one square on the diagram equals one knot, although each knot is made up of two loops. As you work, push loops of knots close together so they completely cover the bearer cord.

Leave the ends of the cords along the left side of the rug about 4 inches long so they can be turned under and tacked down when the rug is finished. Splice the colored jute as necessary, following the instructions opposite.

Next, work nine rows of alternating square knots in natural jute. Make individual square knots, following the bottom diagram at left and using the center cords of adjoining knots as filler cords. After completing the first row, work a second row of knots using the filler cords from the first row, as shown in the top diagram opposite. Continue until you've tied nine rows of knots.

You are now ready to begin the first animal panel. There are five designs for the animal panels and the center design panel that make up the finished rug. Each row of animals is worked twice, so the lower half of the rug is a mirror image of the upper half. The eight animals in each row are worked in alternate directions so each pair of animals faces each other.

To work the animals, refer to the charted designs on page 83. Work the bird panel first, using dark red cord. Then work the crocodile in dark green, the bull in dark brown, the fish in rust, and the llama in dark blue. Each band, worked in Cavandoli stitches, is 14 rows deep. To begin, staple a length of colored jute about 2 yards long to the plywood and work the first row of the panel entirely in horizontal double half-hitch knots (see diagrams on page 83). On the second row of the panel, begin working the pattern, counting knots carefully so they correspond to the charted designs.

Work the pattern as it is shown in the chart, and then flop the chart so the next animal faces the opposite direction from the first one, as shown in the photograph on pages 78 and 79. Work the entire chart again (in reverse). Continue working the animal blocks alternately across the width of the runner as many times as necessary. Splice cords whenever necessary.

Separate each band of animals with nine rows of alternating square knots, following the directions above. After working six bands of square knots (counting from the top of the runner), work the center.

The Tree of Life design in the center panel of the rug is 33 rows deep. The diagram on page 83 shows the first 16 rows of the pattern and the seventeenth, center, row. It also indicates the first two repeats of the motifs. Work the chart as indicated eight times across the rug, making 16 tree motifs.

Work the first two rows of the center panel in rust, stapling the colored bearer cord to the plywood on the left of the rug immediately below the last row of square knots in the band of alternating square knots that precedes the center design. Work horizontal half-hitches in natural jute over the bearer cord, and vertical half-hitches in the colored cord over the natural cords, as indicated on the diagram.

After the first two rows, work five rows of dark red, five of dark green, and three of dark blue, following the chart on page 83. Work the next two rows of rust to finish the first half of the center panel. To complete the entire design, reverse the order of the first 16 rows and finish the pattern so the bottom half of the panel is a mirror image of the top half. Start colored bearer cords (for the vertical half-hitches) by stapling them to the board at the left side of the runner. Splice cords when necessary.

When the center panel is finished, work nine rows of alternating square knots, following directions above. Then work the second half of the rug as for the first, reversing the order and working the animals from bottom to top so they point in toward the center of the rug, as shown in the photograph on pages 78 and 79. In other words, work
continued

Alternating square knot

Splicing Macrame Cords

Because of the size of this project, it's impossible to work with cords cut to the length of the rug itself. Even tying the cords into butterfly knots (as is usually done) becomes too cumbersome and time-consuming. Instead, work with pieces of cord no longer than 2 yards and splice each cord when it becomes short enough to need replacement. The procedures for adding new cords vary according to the type of knots being tied.

On Cavandoli-stitched bands, when a cord runs short, plan the knotting so you can tie in a new cord when the short cord (the one you're going to drop) *is going to be a knotting cord rather than a bearer cord.* Drop the short cord and tie in the new cord with a double half-hitch, as shown in the center diagram at right. Leave a tail about 2 inches long at the end of the cord to tuck to the back of the rug; tie it to the dropped cord when the rug is finished.

In alternating square-knot bands, replace a cord when it is a *filler cord in a square knot rather than a knotting cord,* as shown in the bottom diagram at right, by simply laying in a new cord. If desired, trim half the ply from the old and new cords, glue, and wrap with thread, as shown in the diagram on page 58.

After completing the rug, turn it over and tie loose ends of all cords; secure the knots to the back of the rug with a dot of fast-drying craft glue. Let dry.

Splicing on Cavandoli bands

Splicing on alternating square-knot bands

Macrame Rug *(continued)*

the llama band first, then the fish, the bull, the crocodile, and the birds. Work nine rows of alternating square knots between each row of animals and following the birds.

End the rug with six rows of the border pattern used at the top of the rug, working the border also in Cavandoli stitches. Follow directions for the border on page 80.

To finish the runner, fold the ends of all the cords under and tack them to the back of the rug with dental floss or carpet thread. Tie the spliced ends together and secure them to the back of the rug with a dot of glue.

If desired, coat the back of the rug with a light layer of liquid latex rug backing to help keep ends secure and make the rug skid-proof. To apply latex, turn the rug wrong side up and tack it to a board with nails, making sure corners are square and the rug is stretched taut. With a narrow paintbrush, carefully brush a thin layer of latex onto the back, following manufacturer's directions. When coating the bands of alternating square knots, skim the tops of the knots with the latex. Don't saturate them; any latex that soaks through to the front of the knots is apt to be visible on the surface of the rug. Allow the rug to dry thoroughly — at least 24 hours — before removing it from the board. Reapply latex when an area becomes worn.

Horizontal double half-hitch

Vertical double half-hitch

Cavandoli work

Cavandoli Work

Cavandoli work is a knotting technique worked in horizontal and vertical bars so it resembles a solid piece of fabric or tapestry (as in the animal and Tree of Life panels in the macrame rug on pages 78 and 79). It consists of one basic knot, the double half-hitch, and its variation, the vertical double half-hitch (see diagrams at left). Usually worked in two colors, the knotting cords of the background and the contrasting bearer cords make the pattern when vertical double half-hitch knots are combined with regular (horizontal) double half-hitch knots. The background of the design is worked in horizontal double half-hitches, while the colored motif is worked in vertical double half-hitches, as shown in the diagram at left. Thus, the patterns are formed by counting number, color, and direction of knots.

Three or more colors may be worked when the colors are contained within their prescribed rows, as in the Tree of Life panel in the center of the rug.

For Cavandoli work, tie the natural (background) knotting cords to a bearer cord and anchor the bearer cord to a stable base, such as a piece of plywood. Then anchor a cord in a contrasting color beyond the left margin of the rug. Carry the other end of the cord straight across the rug, perpendicular to the knotting cords, and anchor it on the right side so it is straight and taut. Following the charted pattern, use the colored cord as a bearer cord for horizontal double half-hitches to form the background of the square, as shown in the diagram at left. To macrame the pattern, use the colored cord as the knotting cord, tying it in a vertical double half-hitch over a natural cord, forming the patterns shown.

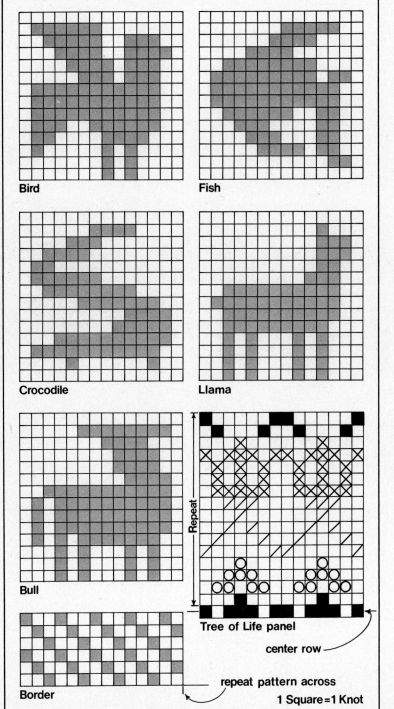

83

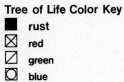

Bird

Fish

Crocodile

Llama

Bull

Border

Tree of Life panel

Tree of Life Color Key
■ rust
⊠ red
⊘ green
○ blue

Repeat

center row

repeat pattern across

1 Square=1 Knot

Woven Stairway Runner

"Rosepath" designs, such as those in the sampler rug, opposite, have been woven in Scandinavian countries for hundreds of years. And while they are traditionally worked on a large floor loom, it's possible to approximate their lovely patterns with a small home-style loom. On pages 86 and 87, there are eight patterns to work into sampler rugs of your own. By making them all the same width but of differing lengths, you can stitch them together into a dramatic stairway runner.

Materials
Two 30-inch artist's stretcher strips
Two 36-inch artist's stretcher strips
8/4 linen thread for warp (see note)
Swedish Berga goat hair yarn in brown and yellow, or a suitable substitute (see note)
4 corrugated fasteners
1 sheet of 10-square-per-inch graph paper
Transparent tape

Directions
Note: To estimate the amount of materials required to make these "mini" rugs, see the directions on page 87. As a general guide, however, plan on using about 3 cones of 8/4 linen and 12 skeins of each color yarn to make small rugs equivalent to 27x72 inches when added together. Although the loom will be warped to be 30 inches wide, the width of the rug will be only about 27 inches when finished.

To begin, build a 30x36-inch frame from the artist's stretcher strips. Stabilize the corners with corrugated fasteners. The 36-inch sides of the frame will be the top and bottom of the loom, around which the warp is wrapped. Along the top of each of these sides, tape a 1-inch-wide strip of graph paper to help mark the spacing of the warps (10 warps to the inch).

To warp the loom, tie the linen thread securely to the bottom of the loom, about 3 inches inside the corner. Warp only the center 30 inches of the frame, leaving a 3-inch margin on each side to make weaving easier. Carry the linen cord up to the top of the frame, around it, and back to the bottom again. Wrap it around the bottom, and carry it back to the top. *Wrap the warp around the frame in a figure-eight pattern* (when viewed from the side). Continue in this way until you've wrapped the frame 154 times, creating 308 warp threads in the 30-inch space. Pull the warp tightly as you wrap around the frame. Knot the ends of the warp string together when necessary; weft yarn will cover the knots. Knot the end of the last warp securely to the frame. Then, with your fingers, space warps along the lines of the graph paper, so there are 10 warps per inch, except on the outside edges where four warps should be grouped together on each side. Be sure to divide the warp threads evenly.

To begin the first "mini" rug, weave with the warp thread to a depth of ½ inch. On the first row, go over and under two threads at a time to establish 150 double-thread warps, except on the selvages; these should be four-thread warps. On the second row, go over the threads you went under on the first row and under those you went over. Continue until you've woven ½ inch. Then switch to yarn for the border strip.

To weave the border, use brown yarn and weave over and under three pairs of warps (6 threads) at a time to a depth of one inch. Begin and end yarn inside the woven area rather than along the selvage. As you weave each row, beat it down firmly against the previous rows by pushing with your fingers, a large-tooth comb, or a dinner fork, making the weaving snug and firm.

To weave in pattern, follow the charted diagrams on pages 86 and 87. The dark areas in the diagrams represent the brown yarn; light areas are yellow. Repeat each pattern as many times as desired. The patterns in the rug shown opposite vary from 12 to 21 inches long, except for pattern number 4, which is worked only once (and can be woven at the top or bottom of an adjoining pattern). When weaving more than one pattern on the loom, separate them with an inch of brown border, following directions above.

At the top of each pattern, end the rug by working two or three rows of linen thread in plain weave over and under pairs of warp threads. Beat them down snugly against previous rows.

To remove the rug from the loom, carefully cut the warp threads from the loom and knot them tightly together as follows: Cut the
continued

Woven Stairway Runner *(continued)*

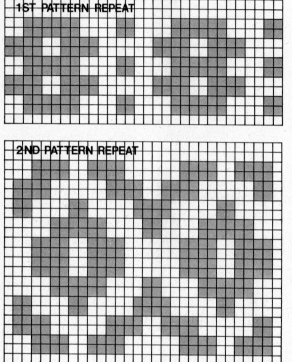

first six threads off the loom. Tie the first five together in an overhand knot. Then cut the next double strands from the loom and tie together one strand from that warp with the one remaining from the previous warp. Continue cutting and tying together strands from adjoining warps until the rug is completely off the loom. Cut threads close to knots, or leave them long for fringe if rugs are not going to be sewn together.

To make the remaining rugs, warp the loom following the directions on page 84. Instead of working ½ inch of linen warp in plain weave, however, work only three rows; then work an inch of brown border, following the directions on page 84. Work the remainder of the rug in pattern, following one of the diagrams.

To assemble the finished samples, stitch them together with strong carpet thread, following directions on page 7 for joining braided rugs. Mount on the stairway with brass rods.

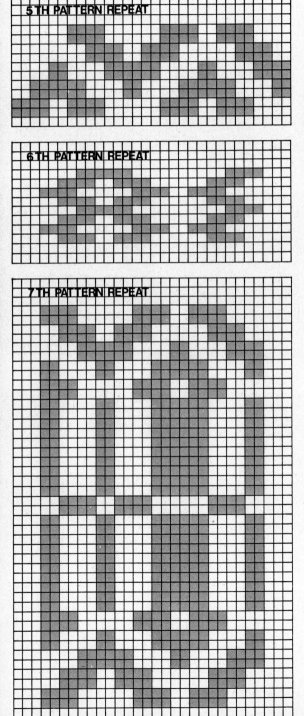

5TH PATTERN REPEAT

6TH PATTERN REPEAT

7TH PATTERN REPEAT

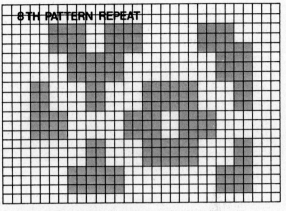

8TH PATTERN REPEAT

1 Row of vertical squares = 1 warp thread

1 Row of horizontal squares = 1 weft thread

How to Estimate Quantities of Yarn for Weaving

To estimate for warp threads: First, count the number of warps (selvage threads) on the loom, or multiply the width of the weaving by the number of warps per inch. Then add to that number any extra threads for special purposes. For example, if you are double-warping the loom, then double the amount you've figured so far. Multiply this number by the length (in inches) of the warp (from the top to the bottom of the loom). Then divide that number by 36 to convert inches into yards. Finally, add a little extra for waste, to get an estimate of the final amount.

To estimate for weft threads, yarn, or fabric: Measure the width of the weaving you plan and add about 25 percent to determine the length of the weft (crosswise thread) you need for one row of weaving. Then estimate how many rows of weft make up one inch of weaving. (Working a small sample at this point helps.) Multiply the width estimate by the number of rows, and then multiply that total by the length (in inches) of the planned weaving. Divide this final sum by 36 for the approximate number of yards of weft yarn or fabric needed.

Family Portrait Rug

This enchanting rug features a happy combination of two techniques. Here the grass, the puppy, and the children are worked with a latch hook, while the lower but slightly textured background is worked in cross-stitches.

By changing the color of the hair, eyes, or clothing, you can make this rug look like a portrait of your own happy family.

1 square = 3 inches

Materials

32x43 inches #4-count penelope rug canvas
Three 140-yard skeins (or six 70-yard skeins) Aunt Lydia's polyester rug yarn in light blue, or a suitable substitute
320-strand packages of precut latch-hook yarn in the following amounts and colors: 1 red, 1 gold, 1 yellow, 1 purple, 1 royal blue, 1 denim blue, 1 black, 1 tan, 2 cream, 6 white, 1 medium brown, 2 pink, 1 light green, 1 rose, 1 light gray, 1 dark gray, 1 orange, 8 olive green, 1 kelly green, and 1 dark brown
1 yard ⅝-inch-wide pink grosgrain ribbon
Black waterproof marking pen
Light blue acrylic paint
Large paintbrush
Large tapestry needle
Latch hook
Carpet thread
Masking tape
5 yards rug binding
Brown wrapping paper

Directions

Note: The finished size of the rug is 28x39 inches.

To make the rug as shown, use the pattern above. If you wish to change the design to resemble your own family, adapt the pattern by altering the design or by changing the hair color.

To make your own pattern, take a slide photograph of your family and project the image on a wall covered with paper cut to the same size as the finished rug. Trace the image onto paper with a pencil, then go over the lines with a black felt-tip pen so they are easy to see. Transfer the design to rug canvas, following the directions on page 53.

If you use the pattern above, enlarge it to size, following the directions on page 53, and transfer it to brown paper. Go over the design lines with a black pen.

Center the rug canvas atop the pattern and trace the design with a waterproof marking pen. Draw a border around the design, leaving a 2-inch hem margin along each edge. Bind the edges of the canvas with masking tape.

Using a paintbrush and light blue acrylic paint, paint the sky so the white canvas will not show when the sky is stitched.

To work the design, begin with the sky. Cut a 2- to 3-foot length of light blue rug yarn, thread it into a needle, and work the sky in cross-stitches (see the diagram on page 16, if necessary). To minimize distortion of the canvas, work half cross-stitches completely across the canvas in one direction. Then complete the stitch by working back along the row in the opposite direction. Begin and end the yarn by running it through two or three stitches along the back.

When the sky is finished, work the remainder of the design with a latch hook, referring to the photograph for colors. Begin at the bottom of the design by hooking the grass with olive green yarn, and work toward the sky, completing each row before

moving up to the next one. If necessary, see page 44 for directions for latch-hooking.

When latch-hooking the children, use the colors of your choice for hair and eyes. Also change the patterns on the clothing, if desired. Work the children's skin in white, and the dog in cream and beige (or the colors of your own dog).

After finishing the latch hooking, add the hair ribbons to the little girl's hair. Cut the ribbon in half. Then tie each piece into a bow and run a thin piece of yarn

or string through the backs of the ribbons with a large, blunt needle. Use the needle to run the yarn through the canvas to the back. Then tie the yarn in a knot or bow on back of canvas.

Block the finished rug, following the directions on page 55. Then sew rug binding to the canvas along the worked edges. Turn the edges to the back, mitering the corners. Stitch the binding to the back of the rug with carpet thread, making sure edges are secure. Add metal curtain rings for hanging.

Needlepoint Doll House Rugs:
Chinese Design

*This stunning miniature
Oriental rug design is
worked on 18-mesh-
per-inch-canvas to
preserve the intricate
details of the pattern. A
fringe of double half-hitch
knots tied in fine linen
cord provides the
finishing touch.*

Directions

The pattern below represents one quadrant of the finished rug. You
may stitch from the chart, or transfer it to graph paper with colored
pencils, reversing as necessary to complete the design.

Mark the center of the canvas with a waterproof pen and bind the
edges with masking tape to prevent raveling. If desired, mount the
canvas in a needlepoint frame to minimize distortion.

Use one strand of yarn throughout, and begin stitching in the center
of the design if you are working from the chart. Stitch small details in
continental stitches and larger areas in basket-weave stitches (stitch
directions are on page 50).

Block the finished rug, following the directions on page 54. Then
trim the unworked canvas to within ½ inch of the needlepoint and cut
backing fabric to match. With right sides facing, sew pieces together,
leaving one end open. Turn, press lightly, and slip-stitch.

For the fringe, cut two 27-inch pieces of cord and approximately
155 pieces each 2½ inches long. Thread a long piece into a needle and
tie it into a lark's head knot in the corner mesh in the last row of
needlepoint at one end of the rug. Adjust the ends of the yarn so one
end is about 1½ inches long. The longer, outside end will be the bearer
cord for the knots that make the fringe. Tie remaining short cords into
alternate spaces in the canvas along the last row of stitching, making
sure ends are even. Tie all short cords into two rows of knots, as
illustrated on page 92. Repeat for the other end of the rug. To finish,
trim ends evenly.

Materials

11x14 inches #18-count canvas
3-ply Paternayan Persian yarn
   in the following amounts and
   colors (or a similar
   substitute): 14 yards #266
   dark rust, 22 yards #274
   medium rust, 6 yards #287
   light rust, 22 yards #005
   white, 5 yards #314 dark
   blue, 10 yards #380 medium
   blue, 8 yards #381
   medium-light blue,
   and 5 yards #382
   light blue
40 yards fine linen
   macrame cord
   (fringe)
Waterproof marking
   pen
Masking tape
11x13 inches rust
   velveteen
#22 tapestry needle
Colored pencils
   (optional)
Graph paper
   (optional)
Needlepoint frame
   (optional)

Color Key

■ dark rust
▨ med. rust
□ light rust
□ white
▨ dark blue
▨ med. blue
□ med. lt. blue
□ light blue

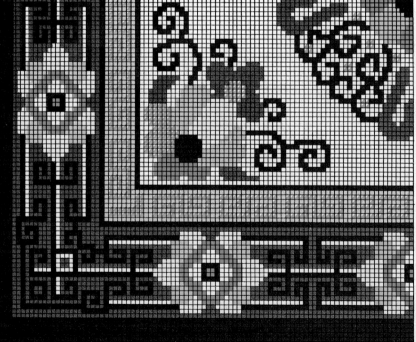

1 Square = 1 Stitch

Needlepoint Doll House Rugs *(continued)*:
Indian Design

The handsome rug opposite is an adaptation of the Navajo "Two Gray Hills" design. Stitched on 18-mesh-per-inch canvas, it works up to 7½ x 10½ inches. To finish the rug, add a fringe worked in double half-hitch knots.

Materials
10x13 inches #18-count canvas
#22 tapestry needle
3-ply Paternayan Persian yarn
  in the following amounts and
  colors (or a suitable
  substitute): 22 yards #050
  black, 22 yards #411 brown,
  8 yards #005 white, 4 yards
  #162 dark gray, and 12
  yards #166 light gray
40 yards fine linen macrame
  cord
Waterproof marking pen
9x12 inches black velveteen
Masking tape

Directions
The pattern, opposite, represents one quadrant of the finished rug. You may stitch from the chart, or transfer it to graph paper with colored pencils, reversing as necessary to complete the design.

Mark the center of the canvas with a waterproof pen and bind the edges with masking tape to prevent raveling. If desired, mount the canvas in a needlepoint frame to minimize distortion.

Use one strand of yarn throughout, and begin stitching in the center of the design if you are working from the chart. If you've made a colored graph of the pattern, you may begin stitching in the upper right corner, but leave approximately 1½ inches of unworked canvas around the design. Stitch small details in continental stitches, and larger areas in basket-weave stitches. For an explanation and diagram of each of these stitches, see page 50.

Block the finished rug, following the directions on page 54. Then trim the unworked canvas to within ½ inch of the needlepoint and cut backing fabric to match. With right sides facing, sew the backing to the needlepoint, leaving one end open. Turn, press lightly, and slip-stitch the opening.

For the fringe, cut two 24-inch pieces of fine linen cord and approximately 130 pieces each 2½ inches long. Thread one of the long pieces into a needle and tie it into a lark's head knot in the corner mesh in the last row of needlepoint at one end of the rug. Adjust the yarn so one end is about 1½ inches long. The longer, outside end will be the bearer cord for the knots that make the fringe. Tie short cords into alternate spaces in the canvas along the last row of stitching, making sure ends are even. Tie short cords into two rows of double half-hitch knots, following the directions below.

Horizontal double half-hitch knot

Making a Fringe with Double Half-Hitch Knots
To make this decorative fringe, first tie on the cords for the knots, as indicated in the directions above and on page 90. The outside cord, number 1 in the diagram at left, should be the longer of the two cords tied in the first knot. It is the bearer cord, around which all of the double half-hitch knots are tied.

Stabilize the rug and bearer cord by thumbtacking them to a cork or macrame board. Tack the bearer cord on the left to hold it in place. Then carry it across the rug and tack it off to the side so it is straight and taut at all times.

For each knot, wrap the end of a short cord around the bearer cord twice, as shown in the diagram (see cord 2). Push loops close together. Then wrap the next knot (with cord 3), using your fingers to snug it close to the previous one. The bearer cord should be completely hidden by the knots that are made over it.

At the end of the first row of knots, unpin the bearer cord, bend it back along the first row of knots, and re-tack it in position for the second row of knots. When all knots are tied, trim fringe to ½ inch so ends are even.

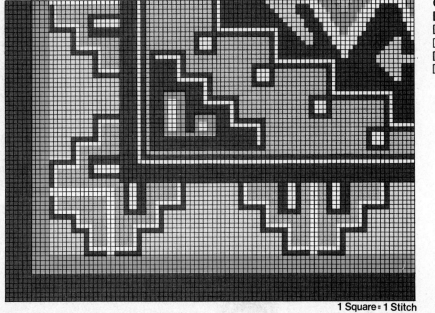

Color Key
- ■ black
- ▨ brown
- □ white
- ▦ dark grey
- ▧ light grey

1 Square = 1 Stitch

Speed-Hooked Rug: Deco Dancers

Our romantic "Dancers" design, opposite, is a punch-needle rug worked with a speed-hooking tool. With this nifty device, you can hook up to a square foot of backing fabric in just an hour or two, making it a real boon to rug crafters with busy schedules.

Materials

Norden Crafts "Eggbeater" speed-hooking rug needle, or a suitable substitute
72x84 inches heavy-duty burlap
Norden Crafts 3-ply wool rug yarn (or a comparable substitute equal in weight to 4-ply knitting yarn) in the following amounts and colors: 18 ounces white, 4 ounces beige, 14 ounces blue, 12 ounces gray, 22 ounces black, 4 ounces green, 4 ounces red, 2 ounces pink, 1 ounce purple, and 12 ounces yellow
Rug frame
Liquid latex rug backing
Waterproof marking pen

Color Key

1 White
2 Beige
3 Light blue
4 Gray
5 Black
6 Green
7 Red
8 Rose
9 Purple
10 Yellow

Directions

Note: The finished size of the rug is approximately 50x75 inches.

Enlarge the pattern below, following the directions on page 53. *Note that the design has already been reversed,* so it can be transferred directly to the rug backing. Transfer it, centered, to the fabric and go over design lines with a waterproof pen so they are easy to see. Mount the fabric, or a portion of it, in the rug frame with the design facing up. The fabric must be taut.

Roll yarn into balls, if necessary, so it will flow freely into the needle as you work. Set the needle for a medium-height loop and thread yarn into it, following manufacturer's directions.

To hook the design, first outline the shapes in the pattern with one or two rows of loops. Then fill shapes with rows of loops hooked back and forth across each area. Work one section of color at a time, following the color key at left.

To work the needle, grasp the handle in your left hand (if you are right-handed) and push the needle into the fabric until the base rests firmly on the burlap. Working with the needle perpendicular to the fabric, turn the handle clockwise, guiding it so it "walks" along the burlap, automatically making loops. When you finish a row, move the needle to the next row, crank the handle counterclockwise, and work back alongside the previous row. With practice, you'll be able to work about a square foot an hour.

Check the front of the rug periodically to make sure that the loops cover the backing completely and that the height is consistent. If you've missed a spot, fill it in when working the next row.

After hooking the rug, remove it from the frame. To finish it, nail or staple it facedown on a board or floor, *making sure corners are square and fabric is taut.* Apply liquid latex rug backing to the hooked area. When latex is dry, trim excess fabric to within 3 inches of the hooked area. Finish the margin of the rug (making a finished edge), following the directions on page 54.

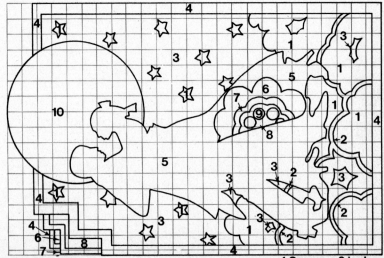

1 Square = 3 inches

We would like to express our appreciation and sincere thanks to all of the people who contributed designs to this book.

Designers

Acknowledgments

Our thanks also go to these people whose creative talents and technical skills were a valuable help to us in producing this book.

Peter Amft, Photographer 95
Mike Dieter, Photographer .... Cover, 4-5, 14,
15, 19, 22-23, 26-27, 41, 49, 51, 56-57, 61,
63, 68, 69, 71, 73, 77, 78-79, 85, 89, 91, 93
Thomas E. Hooper, Photographer 43, 65
William Hopkins, Photographer 13, 17, 21,
29, 31, 32, 33, 36-37, 45, 67, 74
Frank L. Miller, Photographer 47
Dick Swift, Photographer 8-9, 10-11

Blaser/Court Art Studio   Jill Mead
Linda Emmerson   Jessie Walker